Reprint

"Edward" and "Sven I Rosengård"

A Study in the Dissemination of a Ballad

Archer Taylor

Fathom Publishing Company

ISBN: 978-1-888215-69-4
Library of Congress Control Number: 2017962483

First printed by the University of Chicago Press, Chicago, Illinois.

Fathom Publishing Company
PO Box 200448
Anchorage, AK 99520-0448
www.fathompublishing.com
www.archertaylor.com

Archer Taylor

Archer Taylor (center) on an Atlantic cattle boat during a summer trip to Europe during his Swarthmore years.

Archer Taylor (left) with a friend and his sisters.

Introduction to Taylor Reprints

Archer Taylor was born August 1, 1890 and died September 30, 1973. He was called Archer because the family had difficulty agreeing on a name, and his uncle began calling him Sagittarius, symbolized in Greek mythology by the archer—half-man, half-horse in the ninth astrological sign.

Taylor wrote many books and a vast number of articles, some extended studies of the subject at hand and others short notes or queries. He grew up in a world in which academic-minded students learned Latin and Greek in grammar school, and he learned. In the years that followed, he continued to learn. Ultimately he read and spoke thirteen languages, with varying degrees of proficiency to be sure. In high school and early college years at Swarthmore, he worked on a cattle boat to Europe at the start of the summer. Once there, he traveled to the various countries in Europe learning the languages and meeting the people before returning to port to sign on a boat for the trip home. These experiences left him with a love of language and languages (and a life-long dislike for marmalade, pumpernickel and salt pork, the only foods for the crew on the voyage once the fresh things had been eaten). These experiences ended with World War I when he was caught in Europe at the start of the war and had to make his way home. His family sought news of his location and condition in the flyer shown on the next page.

After finishing Swarthmore in three years, Taylor taught and studied, earning his M.A. at the University of Pennsylvania and his PhD at Harvard and publishing his dissertation on the Wolfdietrich epics in 1915. He taught at Washington University in St. Louis starting in 1915, moving to the University of Chicago for the years

Mr. ARCHER TAYLOR,

born August 1st, 1890,
West Chester, Pennsyl-
vania, U. S. of America,
Father, American born Citizen,
Lowndes Taylor, West
Chester, Pennsylvania.

Instructor and Assistant Professor for two years at "State College" Pennsylvania.

Specialty, German Language and literature.

He went to Europe in June 1914, to persue special studies toward his Ph. D degree.

He was last heard from by postal mailed Wilhemlshohe, (Bz. Cassel) Germany.

In that postal he announced his intention to go at once to Gottingen.

He gave his address as "Archer Taylor, Dresden, Poste Restante. Germany.

But he has acknowledged no mail so addressed to him.

He has visited Germany several times on summer tours, and is somewhat familiar with the people and their language.

He speaks also a little French.

He is a graduate of Swarthmore College, a Quaker Institution, and also of the University of Pennsylvania.

He was studying at Harvard University for his Doctor's Degree, and went to Germany sssisted by Swarthmore College.

He had sufficient Credits for ordinary purposes and usual expenses in times of peace.

Please assist him in any way possible, also give any information of him to the German Police, and inform the local American Representatives, (Consul &c.)

Also kindly send information pegarding him to his uncle, Ervine D. York, Flushing, New York.

Or to his father,
Lowndes Taylor, West Chester, Pennsylvania,
U. S. of America.

1925 into 1939. He ended his teaching career at the University of California, Berkeley, where he served from 1939 to 1958 and was chairman of the Department of German from 1940 to 1945. Taylor published *The Proverb* in 1931, followed by *Index to the Proverb* in 1934. His *Bibliography of Riddles* was published in 1939, and a number of other riddle books followed. Archer Taylor and Bartlett Jere Whiting published *A Dictionary of American Proverbs and Proverbial Phrases, 1820-1880* (Cambridge, Massachusetts: Harvard University Press 1958). Although much of his writing concerned folklore, he also wrote *A History of Bibliographies of Bibliographies* in 1955 and *General Subject-Indexes Since 1548* was published in 1966. Other books and an extraordinary number of articles flowed from his ongoing research, and these were the years before computers and word processing. My sister and I remember alphabetizing yellow 2x3 slips he prepared, one for each proverb or riddle.

Taylor married Alice Jones in 1915, and she bore him three children, Margaret, Richard and Cynthia. Alice sadly died early in 1930, and he married Hasseltine Byrd in 1932 and fathered two more children, Mary Constance and Ann.

A collateral benefit of his teaching position at the University of California was that Taylor could send his professional mail through the University. He carried on a prodigious correspondence with individuals and journals of similar interests around the world. When these individuals came to California, they often stopped to visit and to discuss their scholarship. Former students became close friends, illustrated by the friendship between Wayland Hand and Taylor that lasted the rest of Taylor's life. Many of Taylor's letters are collected at universities and some of the collections are available online.

His large library is now with the University of Georgia in Athens, except his ballad collection which is with the University of California, Berkeley. In addition to collecting books himself, Taylor watched for books and collections that he knew were sought by universities around the world. He might buy and send the desired books or notify the university so it could buy them. He was honored after World War II for his extended efforts to rebuild the university library in Dresden.

Wolfgang Meider published one of the reprints of *The Proverb* and posted a Biographical Sketch that included the following:

> In 1960 Archer Taylor was rightfully and deservedly honored by a most impressive "Festschrift" which his two friends Wayland D. Hand and Gustave O. Arlt edited with the befitting title *Humaniora, Essays in Literature, Folklore, Bibliography, Honoring Archer Taylor on His Seventieth Birthday* (Locust Valley/New York 1960). The subtitle summarizes Taylor's three major areas of expertise and such internationally renowned contributors as Bartlett Jere Whiting, L. L. Hammerich, Dag Strömbeck, Stith Thompson, Walter Anderson, Taylor Starck, Kurt Ranke, Lutz Röhrich, Matti Kuusi, Georgios A. Megas, Robert Wildhaber, Francis Lee Utley, Anna Brigitta Rooth, Will-Erich Peuckert, Wolfram Eberhard, Julian Krzyzanowski, etc. acknowledge Taylor's worldwide influence.

Influenced by Wayland Hand, the Western States Folklore Society (formerly California Folklore Society) holds annual meetings to encourage professional and amateur folklorists to meet each other, present papers, and engage in discussions of all aspects of folklore and folklife. Since Taylor's 1973 death, the annual meeting has included the Archer Taylor Memorial Lecture. These lectures often reappear as scholarly articles, something that would have pleased Taylor.

Archer Taylor lived and died with friends around the world. He never passed up opportunities to explain and teach—the difference between anecdote and antidote, for example, when a teenage daughter got it wrong. He generously shared his knowledge and curiosity with all.

Ann Taylor Schwing

February 2018

"EDWARD"

AND

"SVEN I ROSENGÅRD"

THE UNIVERSITY OF CHICAGO PRESS
CHICAGO, ILLINOIS

———

THE BAKER & TAYLOR COMPANY
NEW YORK

THE CAMBRIDGE UNIVERSITY PRESS
LONDON

THE MARUZEN-KABUSHIKI-KAISHA
TOKYO, OSAKA, KYOTO, FUKUOKA, SENDAI

THE COMMERCIAL PRESS, LIMITED
SHANGHAI

"EDWARD"
AND
"SVEN I ROSENGÅRD"

A STUDY IN
THE DISSEMINATION OF
A BALLAD

ARCHER TAYLOR

THE UNIVERSITY *of* CHICAGO PRESS
CHICAGO · ILLINOIS

PIAE MEMORIAE

PREFACE

THE comparative study of the English and Scottish popular ballad, although greatly facilitated by the standard collection of Francis James Child, lingers in the doldrums. No detailed analysis of any ballad has been undertaken by an English or American scholar since the completion of that monumental work; and Child's headnotes—supplemented by the learning of Professor Kittredge in the *Journal of American Folklore* and elsewhere—have remained for thirty years America's sole contribution to the history of ballad texts. Child presents in convenient order the ballad's chief variations in detail, but does not often or consistently make any endeavor to explain the variations, to point out their significance, or to deduce from them the ballad's history. Such an endeavor did not fall within the scope of his plan.

Obviously we must know the history and relations of the existing texts before we can profitably indulge in speculations about ultimate origins. Such speculations, when they occur, have been unduly generous with quotations from ethnological writers on the South Seas and other parts of the globe equally remote from direct connection with the English and Scottish popular ballad. They have totally ignored Scandinavian texts and studies.[1] It is wiser to stay nearer at home and determine, as well as may be, the life-history of a single ballad; to seek the information to be derived from a study of the texts themselves, instead of visiting Malaysia. When we have fuller knowledge of the history of at least a score of important ballads, when we

[1] Exception might be made for Hjalmar Thuren *Folkesangerne paa Færøerne* (1907), but even in this instance acquaintance with the book is superficial.

know how a ballad behaves on the lips of the folk, then we shall have a sufficient stock of information for the ethnologist to take journeys afield.

Comparison and analysis of the English and Scandinavian ballad texts tells us much, but some things must always remain uncertain. In the pages that follow, I often speak of the "original" form and of "original" traits. The word "original" in such contexts is a convenient term to express the fact that comparison permits us to deduce a form from which the existing texts may be derived. The word "original" does not imply my belief that I have attained to the ultimate origin of "Edward" or of perhaps even a single detail in that ballad. The word is merely a convenient way of saying that we cannot see farther back in the history of our present texts. Nor would I for a moment suggest that the summation of the details termed "original" would give us the ballad itself, for the whole is more than the sum of the parts, even if we were sure that we had all the parts at our disposal. Furthermore, we have no guaranty that the parts which we can identify as older all belong to the same level, and hence we dare not combine them. The aim of this comparison and analysis is not to determine as many "original" traits as possible, but to establish the ballad's history and, above all, the manner of its dissemination. It is indeed a desperate undertaking to reconstruct a ballad text,[1] and one hesitates to venture upon so difficult a task. But a systematic comparison and analysis of the variations tells us many things which can be discovered in no other way and leads us to a clearer understanding of the historical development.

Nearly threescore texts have been at my disposal. The

[1] See such brave efforts as those of Sofus Larsen *Niels Ebbesens Vise* (1908), *Ebbe Skammelsøns Vise* (1923), *Fire danske Viser fra Middelalderen* (1923), and E. von der Recke *Nogle Folkeviseredactioner* (1906).

material available for the study of "Edward" has approximately been tripled. At least six or eight additional texts exist, but they are withheld from scholarly use.

This study must necessarily leave untouched a difficult and interesting problem and one of much greater importance than the history of a single ballad. Child recognized that "Edward" belonged to a special type of ballad, a type of which we have but few representatives. These ballads, notably "Lord Randal" and "Edward," employ dialogue to tell the story, but in a way which differs strikingly from that of other ballads. The origin, history, and essential characteristics of this form are entirely unknown.

I am grateful to many friends and well-wishers for assistance in this study, undertaken with the aid of a stipend granted by the John Simon Guggenheim Foundation. This stipend was generously supplemented by the University of Chicago. Kaarle Krohn (Helsinki), with whom I spent the greater part of my time abroad, has given generously of his time and erudition. For these friendly services I am glad to acknowledge my indebtedness.

ACKNOWLEDGMENTS

FOR Swedish texts from Finland I am indebted to Otto Andersson (Åbo). Sverker Ek (Gothenburg) discovered and copied for me an unprinted and previously unknown text from Bohuslän, a region in which the ballad was not known to be current. He also searched for the lost Swedish text of 1640, as did H. Grüner-Nielsen (Copenhagen). For access to the resources of the Dansk Folkemindesamling I am indebted to H. Grüner-Nielsen and Hans Ellekilde, of the Norsk Folkeminnelag to Knut Liestøl and Reidar Th. Christiansen, and of the Västsvenska Folkminnesarkiv to Waldemar Liungman. In this country Robert W. Gordon has searched the Archive of American Folk-Song for me. Arthur Kyle Davis, Jr., and Wirt Cate have done me notable kindnesses. Mr. and Mrs. T. P. Cross have given me an unprinted text. Acknowledgments to various publishers and collectors who have given me permission to reprint texts from their materials are made in each instance, as circumstances demand. To all these friends and helpers I express once more my thanks.

THE STUDY OF THE BALLAD

THE STUDY OF THE BALLAD

O F THE ballad of "Edward," which Child rightly calls "one of the noblest and most sterling specimens of the popular ballad," not very much material is available. Traditional versions are so rare and have been recorded in such a state of corruption that no comparative study can attain to certainty regarding the important details of the story. Yet the situation is not entirely hopeless, for the number of versions, small as it is, is in fact much larger than appears from the standard reference works;[1] and the utter despair voiced by T. F. Henderson, who declared that the only traditional English version known to him was a vulgar debasement of Bishop Percy's text, is quite unjustifiable.[2] As a matter of fact, we have a sufficient stock of versions to warrant reasonable deductions.

So famous a ballad need not be retold in full. A mother catches sight of blood on her son's coat and asks him what it is. At first he evades giving a truthful answer, but ulti-

[1] Very little which calls for notice has been written about "Edward." I take occasion to warn against an essay by Hugo von Meltzl "Eduard der schottischen Ballade Archetypon unter den Széklern nebst Varianten verschiedener Nationen" *Acta comparationis litt. univ.* IV (Kolosvár 1880–81). I have seen the reprint in 29 pages. In this essay "Lord Randal" (Child No. 12) and "Edward" are confused. See the headnotes in Child *English and Scottish Popular Ballads* I 167 ff. and Grundtvig *Danmarks gamle Folkeviser* VI 142 ff.; E. Schmidt "Edward" *Forschungen zur neueren Literaturgeschichte; Festgabe F. R. Heinzel* (1898) 29–50; *Journal of American Folklore* XXXIX (1916) 93.

[2] *Ballad in Literature* (Cambridge 1922) 25. See Taylor "The Texts of 'Edward' in Percy's *Reliques* and Motherwell's *Minstrelsy*" *Modern Language Notes* XLV (1930) 225–27.

mately confesses the murder of his brother. Then follows a series of questions as to what he will do with himself and what will become of his wife, children, and property. In two versions there is a concluding curse implicating the mother in the crime and in others a series of stanzas in which the son declares he will return "when the sun and moon dance on the green . . . . and that will never be."

The most superficial examination of the versions of the ballad reveals the existence of two groups, the Scandinavian and the English. The differences which mark these groups are not merely linguistic, but concern also the ballad's structure and spirit. Although the traits belonging to one group are not found in exactly the same form in the other, the Scandinavian and the English ballads are evidently closely related and the possibility of independent origins need not be discussed.

In comparing these traits one after the other, we are forced to raise each time the question of development or corruption. When the differences are recognized, we can often discover a reason for their existence and can see in which direction change has taken place. After the thorough examination of the ballad has been completed, we may venture to compare as wholes the different types into which the ballad falls. It is not safe or wise to undertake at the beginning such a comparison of the types, since at that stage we shall find it difficult to separate details from matters of greater import. When the details have been disposed of in this fashion, a later summarizing discussion can refer to the previous examination of details and the results gained by it. A final word of explanation regarding the examination of details is appropriate. Each trait is taken up and its variations tabulated. Usually one variation will have impressed itself upon us during the process of tabulation, and we may have acquired some more or less well-founded notion regarding it. This particular variation—or one chosen at random—serves us as a starting-point, and we attempt to arrange all other forms of the traits as its derivatives or, conversely, we seek to show that it is a corruption. If our decision has been at fault we are soon led to correct the error by discovering that the evidence does not agree with our hypothesis.

A characteristic difference between the Scandinavian and the English traditions appears in the introduction to the ballad. This difference is concerned with matters essential to ballad style, and we shall invoke important general stylistic considerations in discovering the relations of the Scandinavian and English poems. The Danish ballad begins:

> GD A 1 Hvor har du været saa længe?
>   Svend i Rosengaard!
> Og jeg har været i Enge,
>   kære Moder vor!
> I vente mig sent eller aldrig![1]

The Norwegian version preserves the rhyme, but is obviously a corruption of the Danish text:

> GN 1 Hor hev du vori saa lengje?
>   I Svenn i Rosensgaar!
> I enge hos drenge,
>   kjær moder vaar;
>   du venter mig sent eller aldrig!

The phrase "hos drenge" has been added to fill out the line. The Swedish versions have no rhyme, e.g.:

> GS C 1 Hvar har du varit så länge?
>   Jag har varit i stallet.[2]

---

[1] All references to texts are made in this manner. The abbreviations are explained in the list of reprinted texts. The defective texts which begin at a later point are not to be taken seriously; see GD B; GS L, M; GSF F.

[2] Cf. GS B 1, C 1, D 1, E 1, F 1, G 1, H 1, J 1, K 1, †N 1; GSF A 1, B 1, D 1, †E 1, †H 1, J 1. Evidently defective or corrupt versions which permit an earlier form to be recognized are marked with an obelus. For comment on GSF H 1 see below, p. 12 n. 2.

A substitution which is found only in Finland replaces the stable by the lake shore:

> GSF G 1 Vart haver du varit så länge?
> Jag har varit vid sjöastrand.[1]

In the absence of any parallel to this scene outside of Finland we may feel little hesitation in rejecting it. No significance appears to attach to the similarity between Finnish and Danish or English tradition in that the murder takes place out of doors.

In the English ballads the abrupt introduction differs strikingly from what we have seen hitherto:

> GE A 1 What bluid's that on thy coat lap,
> Son Davie, son Davie?
> What bluid's that on thy coat lap?
> And the truth come tell to me.[2]

All the English versions begin with this stanza or some obvious modification of it. On the whole the Scandinavian introduction seems probably more original; at least its leisureliness is in keeping with ballad style. Yet it must remain doubtful whether the actual words of the Dano-Norwegian tradition are original, inasmuch as they exhibit a striking resemblance to the beginning of "Den forgivne Datter,"[3] the Danish version of "Lord Randal,"[4] in which ballad this beginning is known all over Western Europe:

> Hvor har du været saa længe?
> Elselille, kær Datter min,
> Og jeg har været i Enge,
> Moder min,
> Jeg har saa ondt, jeg har saa ondt for Hjærtet mit.

This striking resemblance raises at once the question whether the stanza is to be assigned to "Edward" or to

[1] FF A 1, B 1, C 1, D 1; GSF C 1, G 1.

[2] From this point on refrains are ordinarily omitted in quotations.

[3] *Danmarks gamle Folkeviser* No. 341.   [4] Child No. 12.

6

"Lord Randal" and the tenacity with which the "Lord Randal" ballads cling to the stanza makes it certain that the stanza belongs to "Lord Randal." Another fact should arouse our suspicion: with few and readily explicable exceptions, this is the only rhyming stanza in the Scandinavian texts of our ballad. While it is conceivable, but highly improbable, that the rhymes in the remaining stanzas have been lost, the evidence seems to indicate that the introductory stanza to "Sven i Rosengård" has been taken over from another ballad.

I cannot, however, bring myself to a complete and unconditional rejection of this introductory stanza. Although the Scandinavian introduction appears to be borrowed, it may nevertheless be a surrogate for the original introduction. Consequently the Scandinavian tradition in general might represent the original ballad more faithfully than does the English, for the Scandinavian ballad has an introduction—although probably not the true one—and the English has none. Let us set the typical English and Scandinavian texts side by side and examine more closely this possible contamination with "Lord Randal" and the general treatment of the narrative. As examples I select GE A and GS C, since these long and full texts display the differences in narrative technique to excellent advantage:

GE A	GS C
	1 Hvar har du varit så länge? Jag har varit i stallet.
	2 Hvad har du gjort i stallet? Jag har vattat fålarna.
1 What bluid's that on thy coat lap?	3 Hvi är din fot så blodig? Svarta fålan trampa' mig.
2 It is the bluid of my great hawk.	
3 Hawk's bluid was neer sae red.	

7

4 It is the bluid of my greyhound.

5 Hound's bluid was neer sae red.

6 It is the bluid o my brither John.   4 Hvi är ditt svärd så blodigt?
                                            Jag har slagit min broder.

The English versions spring at once into the turmoil of
tragedy, while the Scandinavian versions begin in a state
of rest and gradually lead up to the disclosure. A similar
difference in the story's development is seen in two versions of "Lord Randal."

A   C

1 O where ha you been, Lord
    Randal, my son?
  And where ha you been, my
    handsome young man?
  I ha been at the greenwood;
    mother, mak my bed soon,
  For I'm wearied wi hunting,
    and fain wad lie down.

2 An wha met ye there, Lord
    Randal, my son?
  O I met wi my true-love.

3 And what did she give you?
  Eels fried in a pan.

4 And wha gat your leavins?   1 What's become of your hounds,
  My hawks and my hounds.   King Henrie, my son?
                                      They all died on the way

5 And what becam of them?   2 What gat ye to your supper?
  They stretched their legs out   I gat fish boiled in broo.
    an died.

A survey of the texts shows readily enough that the introduction in A is original, while the abrupt beginning of
C is a secondary development. We note that the static beginning is felt to be a necessity, for C provides such a beginning by interchanging the order of the stanzas. The situation provides an illustration of Olrik's *Indledningslov*,
i.e., of the principle that folk narrative begins with a

situation in a state of calm and develops it into a state of conflict.[1] Returning now to the consideration of "Edward," we are more inclined to grant that the form of the Scandinavian ballad is original—whether the details be old or not—while the English ballad has been truncated.

The reader can justly ask what has been gained by the preceding analysis and comparison. The answer is that we have now formed an opinion which further evidence may support and confirm: that the Scandinavian tradition represents an old stage in the history of "Edward." We have also observed that the Scandinavian tradition in its present form has been much altered. Merely as a matter of theoretical interest, we can remember that one of the arguments used was derived from the structural and aesthetic principles of Axel Olrik. We are not restricted to purely numerical calculations in our study.

When we take the next step in our comparison a difficult question confronts us, and a question which must be answered by means entirely different from those which we have just employed. In Swedish and Finnish tradition the second stanza often contains a question which follows logically on the mention of the horse-stable in the first stanza and which indeed takes up the word itself, e.g.:

> GSF A 2 Vad haver du gjort i stallet så länge?
> Jag haver skrapat blacken.

The English tradition, which begins at a later point in the story, knows nothing of this question. The Dano-Norwegian tradition is equally ignorant, since it, too, leaps at once from describing the scene to revealing the tragedy. Consequently if we accept this detail we must rely on

---

[1] *Nogle Grundsætninger for Sagnforskning* ("Danmarks Folkeminder" [Copenhagen 1921] XXIII) 77 §76.

Swedish and Finnish tradition, where, however, the evidence is not unambiguous. Here we have to discuss two possibilities: either a detail is lost in transmission or it has developed and has found a place in the ballad as an element which a later singer has felt to be essential. If we can find that the detail under discussion is, notwithstanding a superficial relevancy, imperfectly fitted into the ballad, we shall have explained the development. If we fail in such an endeavor, we must conclude that the detail is properly a part of the ballad. The imperfection may show itself in many ways—stylistic, verbal, and logical. In looking for the imperfection we may become convinced and may find arguments to prove that after all no imperfection exists and that consequently the ballads lacking this detail are defective. Our examination must be carried on with an open mind, ever ready to discard a hypothesis for the direct opposite. Of course it is rendered simpler by the fact that only two possibilities need be considered—there are only two horns to the dilemma. Before coming to a decision let us set the two Scandinavian forms in parallel:

GD A 1	GS F
1 Hvor har du været saa længe? Og jeg har været i Enge.	Hvar har du vatt så länge? Jag har vatt i stallet.
	2 Hvad har du gjort i stallet? Jag har ryktat hästen.
	3 Hur är din sko så blodig? Jo hästen har mig trampat.
2 Hvorfor er dit Sværd saa blodigt? For jeg har dræbt min Broder.	4 Hur är ditt svärd så blodigt? Jag har stuckit ihjäl min broder.

The essential difference between these two forms lies in the second and third stanzas of the Swedish text, which have no correspondences in the Danish tradition. The following tabulation[1] makes clear the exact situation in the traditional versions:

GSF				
A 1	2	3	4	
B 1	2	3	4	
C 1	–	3	4	
D 1	2	3	4	
E 1	–	3	4	
F –	–	3	4	
G 1	2	3	4	
H 1†	2	3	4	
J 1	–	2^{a}†4^{b}		

GS A (not seen)				
B 1	–	3	4	
C 1	2	3	4	
D 1	2	3	4	
E 1	2	–	4	
F 1	2	3	4	
†G 1	–	†	†	
H 1	–	3	–	
J 1	2	3	4	
K 1	2	3	4	
L –	–	3	4	
†M ?	?	?	4	
N 1^{a}†2^{b}	–	4		

FF A 1	2	3	4
B 1	2	3	4
C 1	2	3	4
†D 1	†	†	†
E 1	–	3	4

GD A 1	–	–	4
†B –	†	†	†

GN 1	–	3	4

It is, I think, sufficiently obvious that "2" depends entirely on what precedes and is merely a logical link in the chain of incidents. Its relation to the adjoining stanzas will occupy us in a moment. The situation regarding "3," which we shall dispose of for the sake of convenience, is altogether different. Several arguments are at our disposal when we examine "3." The most important of these arguments deal with the logic of the narrative and with the state of the texts. When we have "2" present and "3" absent, as in

> GS E 1 Hvar har va't så länge?
> Jag har va't i stallet.
>
> 2 Hvad har du gjort i stallet?
> Jag har vatnat fålar alla.
>
> 3 Hvi är ditt svärd så blodigt?
> Jag slog ihjäl min broder.

we do not hesitate to assume the loss of "3," which would here fall between the second and third stanzas. The dis-

---

[1] In this tabulation the numbers 1–4 refer to the stanzas of the text GS F quoted above, and the superscript letters to the first and second lines of the respective stanzas. For obelus see p. 5 n. 2 above.

closure of the murder is entirely too abrupt, for the de-
layed revealment is an essential characteristic of the ballad. Moreover, such abrupt disclosure as this is found only
in GS E, N, and GSF J, which appear to represent sporadic
accidents of transmission. Accidents of this sort are likely
to occur in any text; but the disruption of these three texts
is so far advanced in other regards that we can safely consider the abrupt disclosure of the murder as an evidence of
decay rather than as an old trait which has been lost elsewhere. GS E exhibits riotous enlargement of the paraphrases in stanzas 6–15 and disorganization of the bequests
in stanzas 5 and 16. GS N exhibits conflation in stanza 1
and serious disorder both in the disclosure of the crime and
in the bequests. GSF J has lost the episode of the bloodstain, which is central in its importance. Inasmuch as these
corruptions in GS E, N, and GSF J are evident without
detailed comparisons, such texts cannot claim to be good
representatives of the ballad tradition. We need not linger
over discarding them, in so far as their testimony concern-
ing the sequence 1, 2, and 4 is concerned.

When we turn our attention to "2," we find several reasons for believing it to be an insertion into the ballad.
Stylistically, "2" differs from the adjoining stanzas. Its
instable form may, furthermore, imply that a gap which
the singers felt to exist at this place in the narrative has
been filled in different ways by different singers. The distribution of the texts in which "2" occurs speaks strongly
against recognizing it as an old element in "Sven i Rosengård." Finally, the stanza "2" is inappropriate on logical
and aesthetic grounds.

The linking of stanzas by the repetition of words, which
is found in the passage from GS E quoted above, and which
is characteristic of all appearances of "2," does not occur
elsewhere in the narrative portion of the ballad. Such

linked stanzas are often produced in the course of oral transmission by the invention of the singers. Hence we are led to conclude that "2" is a late invention, presumably of Swedish make. We observe the rampant growth of such linked stanzas in the paraphrases with which the ballad ends, e.g.:

GS D 11 När skall jag vänta dig igen?
         När korpen han hvitnar.

      12 När hvitnar korpen?
         När svanen han svartnar.

      13 När svartnar svanen?
         etc., etc.

Here, too, the expansion is spurious.

Interesting divergences in the form of "2" seem also to give support to its rejection as a late invention. We find two large groups, one in which the hero waters foals, e.g.:

GS C 2 Hvad har du gjort i stallet?
        Jag har vattnat fålarna.[1]

and one in which he curries a horse, often a gray horse, e.g.:

GSF D 2 Vad haver du gjort i stallet?
         Jag haver ju skrapat Blacken.[2]

Associated with the notion of watering we have always the foals, and with the notion of currying, the horse. In view of this restriction on the words and acts we can with some

---

[1] GS C 2, †E 2, J 2, K 2, N 1; GSF G 2; FF A 2, B 2, C 4. The Swedish *fålarna* probably refers to young horses, not to the foals or colts in the English sense. Since nothing in the argument depends on the distinction, I use *foal* as a convenient equivalent.

[2] GS D 2 (*skådat blacken*), F 2 (*rykat hästen*); GSF †A 2 (*så länge* belongs, of course, to the first stanza), †B 2 (*ryktat brunan*), †D 2 (*Blacken* for *blacken*), †E 1 (stanzas 1 and 2 are contracted into one), †H 1 (stanzas 1 and 2 are conflated and *Blacken* is a proper noun).

show of probability suppose that two traditions have united to form

> GSF A 2 Vad haver du gjort i stallet så länge?
> Jag haver skrapat blacken.
>
> 3 Du är så blodiger på din hand?
> Ja, fålan haver bitit mig.

It seems more than probable that the form in which foals are watered is the earlier invention to fill the gap, for it is both widely known—being reported from Sweden (Bohuslän, Värmland, Östergötland, Södermanland), Swedish Finland, and Finnish Finland—and also old, being found in the first recorded Northern versions (Finnish). The second form, in which a horse is curried, appears to have arisen later in Småland and Blekinge, but, although it propagated itself very successfully in Swedish Finland, it did not reach the Finns.

There remain two further arguments, both of them of considerable weight, for the rejection of "2." The Finnish text (FF E) from central Ingria, which lies in the easternmost part of Finnish-speaking territory, knows nothing of "2." In this it agrees with Western tradition, and an agreement among texts so widely separated geographically seems to preserve an old trait. Finally, we find support in the observation that the menial duties described in "2" cannot possibly have made part of the original ballad.

The presence of "3" alone awakens no feeling of incompleteness and is in keeping with the ballad's spirit as in

> GS B 1 Hvar har du varit så länge?
> Jag har varit i stallet.
>
> 2 Hvarför är din kläder så blodig?
> Hvita folan spjernte mig!

In view, then, of all the arguments which have been brought forward, this order of incidents is original. We are supported in this belief by the English ballads which begin with "3."

We face now questions of the first importance in the ballad's history: In what relations do the diverging Danish and Swedish traditions stand to the English tradition? Has the Swedish ballad inserted both these details or have they been lost in the scantily recorded Danish tradition? In answering these questions certain observations on the spirit of the ballad are helpful. The English story, particularly in the older texts, is seen against a background of court life, while the Scandinavian tradition is laid in a farmstead. The Danish ballad occupies an intermediate position, inasmuch as the farm scene is conceived and presented with less detail than in Sweden or Finland. It needs scarcely be argued that the English ballad preserves here the original state of affairs. We therefore conclude that the tradition has spread from England to Denmark or Norway and thence to Sweden and ultimately to Finland. Yet the implication which such a sketch of the ballad's dissemination might seem to contain, viz., that these two stanzas are to be discarded as modern corruptions and additions, must not be accepted without some further examination of the matter. As we have seen, "2" can be rejected without much hesitation.

Yet "3" must be retained, although Danish tradition, which is represented by a single good text, does not know it. Comparison with the English ballads is instructive:

GS J   GE M

1 Hvar har du varit så länge?
  Jag har varit åt stallet.

2 Hvad har du gjort åt stallet?
  Jag har vattnat hästarna.

15

3 Hvad har du fått på rocken?
   Hästen min har trampat mig.

1 What has came this blood on
   your shirt sleeve?
   This is the blood of the old grey
   horse.

Here we find in both Swedish and English tradition the traits of the coat (shirt sleeve) and the horse, and we can scarcely explain this agreement away as one arising from chance. Details lost in the Danish ballad are preserved in Swedish tradition, although sadly altered in spirit.

The reader will observe the arguments employed in the preceding discussion: in the case of an incident which is a member of a series we cannot discuss the incidents singly. The whole series of events which leads up to the confession must be examined at one time. Arguments drawn from what we know to be the conventional manner of handling such a series can be safely employed. We must, furthermore, be ever conscious that the parallel construction of incidents and their arrangement in a logical series makes easy the introduction of new matter.

The next stanza reveals or at least begins to reveal the murder: blood is seen on the murderer's person or on his sword. In the former event, disclosure is relatively slow; in the latter, disclosure follows immediately. We have accordingly to examine these two forms more closely. The sequence of the first four stanzas in Swedish and Finnish tradition has just been studied, and a minute examination will provide a safe foundation for the comparison.[1] In the Swedish and Finnish ballads blood or dirt is seen on the person and then on his sword in all except defective texts.[2]

---

[1] We may note that a somewhat similar incident occurs in the Halewijn cycle (see Child I 168 n.*), but no relationship appears to exist between it and the disclosure of the murder in "Edward."

[2] GS B 2–3 (*kläder, skjorta*), C 3–4 (*fot, svärd*), D 3–4 (*fot, svärd*), F 3–4 (*sko, svärd*), J 3–4 (*rock, skjorta*), K 3–4 (*byxera, skjurta*); L 2 (*hand*), M(?); GSF †A 3–5 (*hand, arm, svärd*), B 4 (*rock, skjorta*), C 2–3 (*hand, svärd*), †D 3–4 (*skjorta,*

In view of the small number and the nature of the texts which mention only the sword,[1] we need not hesitate to consider them defective. They cannot be grouped with those English ballads which also contain only the sword and thus be regarded as establishing an original form with the sword alone. There is no significant similarity between these particular Scandinavian and English texts.

On examining the tabulation more closely it becomes apparent that where *skjorta* appears in the Swedish texts (from Sweden only) it stands in the last place[2] and the sword is not mentioned. This series is obviously a corruption in which the sword is eliminated. We need not stop long to prove it a corruption: clearly (1) "Why do you have blood on your coat [clothes, trousers]?" (2) "Why do you have blood on your shirt?" cannot reasonably form a climax. The disappearance of the sword is readily comprehensible in these texts which breathe the air of peasant life. For obvious reasons—the presence of the sword in both English and Scandinavian tradition as well as its logical necessity—it cannot be discarded.

We have therefore to consider seriously only texts of the types *hand, sword*[3] and *coat, sword*,[4] and in doing so we may

gjort av din broder), E 2–3 (*skjorta, värja*), F 1–2 (*skjorta, svärd*), G 3–4 (*hand, svärd*), H 2–3 (*skjorta, värja*); FF A 3–4 (*coat, sword*), B 4–6 (*back, foot, sword*), †C 7 (*coat*), E 3–5 (*boots, sword*). The question mark indicates uncertainty as to the text. The incident is lacking in GS G, H; GSF J.

[1] GS E 3; GN.

[2] GS B (*kläder, skjorta*), J (*rock, skjorta*), K (*byxera, skjurta*). In GSF B *skjorta* alone is mentioned and we can no longer tell whether we have here a corruption of the preceding series or, what is more likely, a corruption of the characteristic Finno-Swedish *skjorta: svärd*. The arrangement *skjorta, gjort av din broder* in GSF D is obviously corrupt.

[3] GS C (*foot*), D (*foot*), L (*hand* only), M(?); †GSF A, C, G (*foot*); †FF B. The trait *foot* arises from the conception of the verb *træde* (or its synonyms) as 'trample,' and thereby involves ideas concerned with the stable. The obvious parallelism with *hand* no doubt contributed its share. Whatever the original may have been, *foot* is a later replacement.

[4] GS B, F (*shoe*), J (*coat, shirt*), K (*trousers, shirt*); GSF B (*shirt* only), †D

now reckon all texts containing *shirt* as examples of the second type. In considering these two types it seems more probable that *coat, sword* is older, since *hand, sword* could develop out of it by virtue of the obvious association of *hand* and *sword* while a substitution in the reverse sense is less readily understood. But in such matters we cannot be certain.

In the North, blood is seen on the murderer's coat and sword, while English tradition varies, naming either the sword[1] or the coat (or hand),[2] but with one exception never both in the same text. Two ballads throw light on this dark question: GE E and F, which are contaminated with "The Twa Brothers" (Child No. 49). The former reads:

> GE E 12 O what blude's that upon your brow?
> It is the blude o my gude gray steed.
>
> 13 O what blude's this upon your cheek?
> It is the blude of my greyhound.
>
> 14 O what blude's this upon your hand?
> It is the blude of my gay goss-hawk.
>
> 15 O what blude's this upon your dirk?
> It is the blude of my ae brother.

This elaborately developed incremental repetition, in which both the position and the alleged nature of the bloodstain vary from stanza to stanza, is not found elsewhere. I shall not maintain that the form of GE E and F gave rise, on the one hand, to the Swedish series (*coat, sword*), which concerns itself solely with the position of the bloodstain, and, on the other, to the English series (*steed,*

(*shirt*, "done by your brother"), FF A (*jacket, sword*), C (*coat* only), E (*boots*). On GSF B see the remarks in the second preceding note. The trait *shoe* (*boots*) has arisen in the same way as *foot*; see the preceding note.

[1] GE B, D, I, L, P, Q, R, S. On GE E see the immediately following remarks. GE C, H, K, and O are defective.

[2] GE A, F, J, †M, †N, T, †U.

greyhound, goss-hawk), which concerns itself solely with the nature of the stain. Yet it seems probable that the structure of GE E resembles that of the hypothetical original. Of this original, Swedish and Scandinavian tradition preserve incremental repetition so far as the coat and sword are concerned, while the animals have disappeared; on the other hand, English tradition preserves either the coat or the sword and with the one which is retained, the animals. Although this relationship cannot be regarded as demonstrated, it seems the most satisfactory explanation of the now available facts. More texts might make it possible to answer the questions at issue. As it is, we grope in the dark. Yet there are some indications which favor the explanation which has been given. We have observed that English and Swedish tradition cling tenaciously to the coat:

GE A 1 What bluid's that on thy coat lap?

and

GS J 3 Hvad har du fått på rocken?

as well as to the sword, e.g.:

GE B 1 Why dois your brand sae drap wi bluid?

and

GS D 4 Hur är ditt svärd så blodigt?

The elaborate structure of GE E and F is not readily explicable unless we see in it a relic of an older form, and such an opinion might find some slight support in the almost equally elaborate structure of GSF A. Both of these texts are relatively well preserved and may fairly claim our respect.

The episode in which the blood is declared to belong to various animals is unknown in Scandinavia. For obvious reasons this episode is narrated in stanzas exhibiting incremental repetition, and since the form is relatively well preserved, incremental repetition has probably existed in this section since the ballad's beginnings. A tabulation of the animals mentioned follows:

```
        GE  A B†C  D  E   F G* H  I  J †K  L M N†O †P* Q* R  S T †U
hawk ...  2 1 -  -  14 22 ‡ -  -  -- - ---- †1 †1  1  -  --
hound...  4 -- 16 13 18 ‡ 8  -  1  - †1 3 1  -  -  -- †1 †2 -
horse....   - 2 -  -  12 20 ‡ -  10 †2 -  - 1 2  -  -  --  -  --
```

*GE G 8 (*rabbit*), 9 (*squirrel*); GE P (*crane*); GE Q (*crow*); see comment below.

These three creatures, hawk, horse, and greyhound, are mentioned in the more important uncontaminated versions (GE A, B, J). Each variant names only two animals, and curiously enough the three possible pairs which could be chosen are represented. For a moment one might suspect that no version preserved the original state and that each had lost a member of the trio. But so easy an explanation cannot be correct, for incremental repetition occurs in triplicate and the third member provides the climax. Hence the series must run: blood of hawk (or hound), horse, and brother. Clearly the horse cannot be rejected, since it occurs in GE B, E, F, I, J, M, and N, and, although with a different function, is firmly established in Scandinavian tradition. The only question which arises is whether the hawk or the hound is original. We decide in favor of the hawk because the substitution of the hound would be almost inevitable when hawking fell into disuse.[1] In other

[1] The same alteration is seen in "The Broomfield Hill" (Child No. 43) where we read:

> D 11 "Then whare was ye, my bonnie grey hound,
>   That I coft ye sae dear,
>   That ye didna waken your master,
>   Whan ye kend that his love was here?"

> 12 "I pautit wi my foot, master,
>   Garrd a' my bells to ring,
>   And still I cried, Waken, gude master,
>   For now is the hour and time."

[Footnote continued on following page]

words, the conventional "hawk and hound" (GE A) and "horse and hound" (GE J) have replaced the original "hawk and horse" as found in GE B. A development in the reverse direction is difficult to imagine.

The complete absence of the hawk in Scandinavian tradition need not deter us in reaching this conclusion. Notwithstanding the importance of hawks in Northern commerce they do not appear to be conventional stage property in the ballads.[1] The disappearance of the hawk in Scandinavian ballads on our theme is therefore readily intelligible.[2] It was no doubt facilitated by the natural tend-

---

The second stanza shows complete confusion: the horse should stamp its foot and the hawk should ring its bells.

We see how readily the association of hawk and hounds presents itself from two stanzas of "Lord Randal" (Child No. 12):

> A 4 "And wha gat your leavins, Lord Randal, my son? . . . .
> My hawks and my hounds. . . . .
> 5 And what becam of them, Lord Randal, my son? . . . .
> They stretched out their legs and died. . . . ."

No other text of the ballad mentions the hawks and even here they are surely out of place.

[1] See for comment on hawks and hawking Voionmaa *Suomen Museo* (Finskt Museum) XX (1913) 20–21; Falk "Die altnordischen Namen der Beizvögel" *Germanica: Festschrift für E. Sievers* (Halle a.S. 1925) 236–46 and the literature there mentioned. I have not seen L. Magand d'Aubusson's *La fauconnerie au moyen âge et dans les temps modernes* (Paris 1879). Souhart (*Bibliographie générale des ouvrages sur la chasse* [Paris 1886]) does not, at least at first glance, offer much to follow up.

[2] A similar accident appears to have overtaken the hawk in "Elveskud" (*DgF* 47; "Clerk Colvill" Child No. 42). In the oldest text the hawk and hound appear:

> A 41 "Haffuet hand nu kierer synn høgg och syn hund,
> ind han haffuer syn vnge brud."

So far as my survey of the texts printed in *DgF* goes, the hawk occurs again only in V 15; see also the Swedish texts cited in the long supplementary note to "Elveskud" (*DgF* IV 860, note on B 19). In the later texts, beginning even with Syv (B 19) in 1695, the horse appears and finally runs riot. There are also some curious corruptions of *hund*, which ultimately yields its place to *lund*; see, e.g., K 23, M 22, and other texts. The development appears to have been the replacing of *høgg* by *hest* and later the disappearance of *hund* so that in the late traditional versions both the original animals have vanished.

ency of oral tradition which we find exemplified in the later English texts: a constant pressure to simplify the structure of the ballad brings about the reduction of this episode so that only one animal is mentioned.[1] It is also worth mentioning that the hawk occurs only in the older English texts: only GE A of 1827, B of 1765, E of 1827, and F of 1825 know it. Not a single text taken down in the last hundred years has kept the hawk, although there are traces in the Virginia tradition. The figure of the hawk was evidently passing from the stage at the time when the ballad was first recorded. The substitution of the hawk for either the horse or the hound, if those two animals were original in the ballad, is unlikely. The oldest forms of the ballad are accordingly those current in England.

The animals named in the English versions of the ballad reveal some interesting facts. The fuller texts GE E and GE F, which name all three creatures (horse, hound, and hawk), are expansions under the pressure of parallelism and convention, and since the hawk, the least of three, stands in the last place in an emphatic position, the texts are disordered. The extension of the adjectives shows the enormous influence of analogy and parallelism in determining this passage: the greyhound gives rise to a gray steed and even to a gray hawk (GE F).[2] The greyhound alone is found in GE D and H, apparently, as the result of the reduction of the series. The rabbit and squirrel of GE G show an accommodation to childish interests.

In England as well as in Scandinavia the victim is ordinarily the brother. Yet Swedish tradition names the sister more than once:

[1] See, e.g., GE D, H, I, L, etc.

[2] Cf. also the gray mare in GE J. No doubt the "gay goss-hawk," a conventional phrase, of GE E has played its part in this corruption. Cf. also "The Gay Goshawk" (Child No. 96).

> GS K 4 Hvad har du fått på skjurta?
> Ja ha slakte syster![1]

No one will imagine for a moment that this variation, which has not extended itself beyond Southern Sweden, is more than a chance substitution arising from the obvious association of brother and sister. It is not impossible that some version of a ballad belonging to the Halewijn cycle has aided in this substitution,[2] but I see no verbal similarities or other evidence pointing in this direction. In whatever way the substitution has come about it took rise in one of the three adjoining Swedish provinces, Småland, Östergötland, and Södermanland,[3] and did not extend farther. The existence of so few versions does not justify us in positively dating this substitution, but it seems to be late in the history of the tradition. Similarly Bishop Percy's text, which reads

> GE B 3 Your steid was auld, and ye hae gat mair.
> O I hae killed my fadir deir!

exhibits another substitution. We can have no hesitation in definitely rejecting Henderson's previously mentioned assertion that modern English tradition—or perhaps Motherwell's version (GE A) alone—springs from Bishop Percy's text.[4] Modern English tradition as well as Motherwell's text has preserved the original trait, while Bishop Percy's source introduces, as any ballad singer may do on occasion, an individual variation.

Mention of the brother's body occurs but rarely, e.g.:

> GS D 5 Hvar har du gjort af brodren din?
> Han ligger utom stallsvägg.[5]

[1] See also GS J 4, †M 4.

[2] See Child I 36, 38, and particularly 168 n. 4.

[3] The versions recorded in Södermanland (GS J) and Östergötland (GS K) are practically identical.

[4] See above, p. 3 n. 2.   [5] See also GS F 5.

23

The trait may have been added at a later time as a logical step in the action, although one cannot insist upon such a decision in view of the insufficient evidence.

Various texts give an explanation of the quarrel, but their number is too few and their distribution too scattering for us to reach any final or convincing decision regarding the details. Certainly, the Finnish explanation

> FF B 6 Why did you stab your brother?
> Because he put my wife to shame.[1]

may be rejected without much hesitation. It is, to be sure, conceivable that so important an original trait has been lost, in English tradition as well as in the relatively abundant ballads of Swedish tradition, on which Finnish singers were so closely dependent, but such an explanation is very improbable. Finnish tradition does not seem to preserve any other ancient bit of the story; in fact, it does not preserve the story as a whole with particular faithfulness. One is more inclined to believe that some Finnish singer inserted this explanation, possibly borrowing it from another song, in order to complete the story. If we surrender this explanation, we are left with the one in

> GE A 7 What about did the plea begin?
> It began about the cutting of a willow wand
> That would never been a tree.[2]

This explanation may be a fragment, a substitute for some more intelligible motive, or even the original form. In any event, we cannot re-create the original with any confidence. The omissions, losses, and corruptions exemplified by our texts are quite in keeping with what we might expect. Ballad style gives the advancing stages of the action in high light and does not linger over or preserve explanatory details. Of course, the readiness with which details and even essential matters are lost increases with the de-

[1] Cf. FF C 9.   [2] See also GE C 1, J 4, L 3, M 6, N 4, O 1, †P 3, †T 4.

generation of a ballad, and "Edward," we must remember, has been recovered only in the last stages of decay.

Thus far we have examined in detail only the episode of the murder, the first of the larger parts into which the ballad divides itself. The second part concerns the punishment which falls upon the murderer. Tradition differs sharply regarding this point. In the Scandinavian ballads the murderer takes flight or goes into exile, e.g.:

> GD A 3 Hvor vil du dig hen vende?
> Jeg vil af Landet rende.

The Swedish texts have no rhyme:

> GSF A 6 Vart skall du taga vägen?
> Jag maste rymma landet.[1]

or create a new form, e.g.:

> GS J 5 Hvad skall du ha för detta?
> Jag skall rymma ur riket.[2]

In recasting the stanza the Småland version shows that the singer conceived the situation as utterly ignoble flight:

> GS L 3 Hvart will du fly och vandra?
> Der ingen mig kan klandra.[3]

In Finland, too, the idea is clearly flight (*joutua*), although the Swedish texts taken down in Finland still keep the characteristic phrase *rymma landet*. The vague and shifting distinction between flight and exile makes any tabulation or critical examination impossible. Yet we may perhaps see here a progressive degeneration in the Eastern transmission. It is in any event a matter of the first importance to note that the Scandinavian versions indicate that the punishment is death, for the murderer will not return until Judgment Day.

[1] GS B 4, C 5, E 4, H 3; GSF A 6, B 5, †C 4, F 3, †H 4, J 3.

[2] GS D 6, J 5, †K 5.

[3] Presumably this variation occurs also in GS M. The presence of rhyme marks the stanza as an interloper.

Most of the English ballads[1] employ a very interesting medieval punishment:

> GE A 9 I'll set my foot in a bottomless ship,
> And ye'll never see mair o me.

Still more explicitly we read:

> GE D 19 Ye'll put me in a bottomless boat,
> And I'll gae sail the sea.

The variation in Bishop Percy's version is instructive:

> GE B 4 And whatten penance will ye drie for that?
> Ile set my feit in yonder boat,
> And Ile fare ovir the sea O.

In this situation penance is not the right word and the seemingly obvious implications of exile are not to be taken literally. These notions of penance or exile, whether imposed by self or by law, could hardly have developed into the notion of legal execution by exposure in a bottomless boat. But a development in a contrary direction is readily enough conceived as a weakening of the original situation and as a failure to grasp the irony of the son's remark. If this point be granted, we must then reappraise Bishop Percy's text. If we try to insert the notion of execution into Bishop Percy's text, the elaborate and beautiful metrical structure is necessarily destroyed. Yet we have agreed that exposure in a bottomless boat inheres in the theme. Consequently Bishop Percy's text of "Edward" cannot be the original version of the folk song. In other words, we have in Bishop Percy's text a revision of a folk song, a rewriting which we can justly compare with Goethe's "Heidenröslein."

In the matter of the difference between exposure and exile there can be no reasonable doubt. Punishment by

---

[1] GE A 9, B 4, D 19, †E 16 (*saddle my steed*), †F 23, H 11, I 13, J 5, K 1, L 4, M 7, N 5, O 2, P 6, Q 3, R 3, S 3, T 5.

exposure in a bottomless boat is appropriate to such crimes as fratricide: "Pro crimine flagitiosissimo," says the *Vita Offae secundi* of þryð's punishment, "in navicula armamentis carente apposito victu tenui ventis et mari exponitur condemnata."[1] The clause "And I'll gae sail the sea" is original, since the Scandinavian ballads have developed the notion of exile from it.[2] It must be construed ironically, but when punishment by exposure in a bottomless boat ceased to be employed or understood—and even in the thirteenth[3] century William of Malmesbury[3] found it cruel and unusual ("inaudito crudelitatis modo")—the irony necessarily lost its point.

The clause then finds a literal interpretation:

GE I 13 I'll set me foot on yon shipboard,
    And I'll hope she'll sail wi me.

14 What will ye do wi your bonny bonny young wife,
    Dear son, come tell to me
    I'll set her foot on some other ship
    And I hope she'll follow me.

[1] See K. von Amira "Germanische Todesstrafen" *Abhandlungen der bayrischen Akademie* XXXI (1920–22) No. 3 (1922) 144 ff., 194, 217. We need not take up here the interesting questions touching the origin of this punishment and its possible relations to the burial of the dead in a boat; see M. Ebert "Die Bootfahrt ins Jenseits" *Praehistorische Zeitschrift* XI–XII (1919–20) 179–96; Major "Ship Burials in Scandinavian Lands and the Beliefs That Underlie Them" *Folk-Lore* XXXV (1924) 112–50. We may see a special variation of this punishment in the *bateaux à soupape*, in which so many were drowned that the waters of the Loire were poisoned; see *L'intermédiaire des chercheurs* LXVI (1912) 185,250,294; LXIX (1914) 496; Saint-Edme *Dictionnaire de la pénalité* (Paris 1829–34) IV 428–29.

[2] I am not sure that I see the full significance in the ballad's history of the variations GE H 11[4] "And swim to the sea-ground" and GE J 5[4] "And sail the ocean round." Are we to suppose the former to be original? Certainly the case would not be lacking in arguments to support it: the first form makes sense and is found in an old version (at least a relatively old one, for no version claims great age), while the second form is nonsense and of no particular antiquity. In any event the comparison shows that the true meaning of the passage was still understood by the singer of GE H, although it does not establish that these words belong to the original ballad.

[3] *De gestis reg. Angl.* ii. 139; ed. Stubbs, I 156. See von Amira 144; and in general A. de Cock *Volkssage, Volksgeloof en Volksgebruik* (Antwerp 1918) 83; Taylor "Aussetzung im Boot" *Handwörterbuch des deutschen Märchens* I (1930).

It is not impossible that "yonder ship," "yonders boat," and the like are ultimately corruptions of "bottomless boat";[1] compare, e.g.:

> GE O 2 What will you do when your father comes home,
>   My son, pray tell it to me?
>   I'll put my foot on yonders boat
>   And sail all over the sea.

The same literal interpretation is seen in

> GE J 5 O what will you tell your father dear
>   When he comes home from town
>   I'll set me foot in yonder ship,
>   And sail the ocean round.
>
>   6 Oh what will you do with your sweet little wife
>   Pray son, now tell to me.
>   I'll set her foot in yonder ship,
>   To keep me company.

In these last examples the influence of parallelism extends itself over the first clauses of the will and brings confusion to the narrative.[2] The wife should receive the first bequest and instead she becomes the murderer's companion in exile. The ease with which this confusion arises is shown by its appearance, quite independent of English tradition, in

> GS M 6 Hvad vill du göra af hustrun din?
>   Jo, jag vill ta 'na med mig.

Probably this silly notion of the wife accompanying the husband into exile on shipboard has been transferred from such stanzas as

> GE O 3 What will you do with your children, my son,
>   My son, pray tell it to me?
>   I'll leave them with you, dear mother,
>   To keep you company.

[1] See also such texts as GE P 6 ("yonder hill" has arisen by parallelism), S 3 (like P 6), T 5.

[2] The complete list of texts in which this has occurred is GE I 14, J 6, N 7, O 5, P 6, Q 4, R 4, T 6.

The final stage, in which the punishment becomes merely flight, is found in certain English versions as well as in Scandinavia, e.g.:

> GE E 16 I'll saddle my steed, and awa I'll ride,
> To dwell in some far countrie

and

> GE F 23 This country I maun flee.[1]

This agreement of English and Scandinavian tradition does not mean that an old trait is here preserved. In both regions the progress of corruption—a corruption occasioned by the disuse of the punishment—comes to a similar end.

After announcing that he is going into exile the son makes a nuncupative will and follows it with a series of paraphrases for "never" which answer a question regarding his return. A number of versions have only the paraphrases and make no mention of the will. Although both conclusions make an effective ending to the ballad it seems clear that the will is the proper ending, accompanied, it may be, by the paraphrases. Whether the paraphrases are really necessary is a question which must be left undecided for the moment. A Swedish version shows that the singer regarded the will as essential to the story, for he returns to it after a lapse of ten stanzas. This version also shows how readily the "never" phrases creep into the ballad. The text is as follows:

> GS E 4 Hvad vill du nu då göra?
> Jag rymmer utaf landet.
>
> 5 Hvar vill du göra af hustru och barn?
> De få gå verlden af och an.

---

[1] See also GE N 5. Scandinavian parallels have been given above.

6 När får jag dig hemventa?
  När kyrkan blir enka.

[Nine more such stanzas follow.]

16 Hvar will du göra af åker och äng?
   Den får bli utan hägn och stägn.[1]

The singer remembered when he had finished the paraphrases that the will belonged to the story and added it in a most inappropriate fashion. Since the implication in both the will and the paraphrases—at least so far as the Scandinavian texts are concerned—is that the son will never return, one motif could and did upon occasion crowd out the other.

The bequests, although tradition deals severely with them, appear to concern the wife, the children, and the property, and this situation is so natural that we need not hesitate to accept it as original.[2] In the following tabulation we can survey the considerable variations in matters of detail:

Wife.—She may either be left in grief[3] or told to earn her livelihood by spinning.[4] Begging properly belongs to the children and is assigned to the wife only in company with the children, e.g.:

[1] This imperfect rhyme is not evidence that the Swedish texts once possessed rhymes.

[2] The bequests are lacking in GE D, E, F, G, H, L, M, S; GN; GS B, H, J, K; GSF E, F, G, H. No importance attaches to the fragments FF D; GD B; GE C, K, U; GS G.

[3] FF B 10 var.; GE A 10; GS D 7, F 7. In GS M 8 the trait is assigned to the mother and not to the wife, but this situation is obviously owing to confusion.

[4] FF C 12; GD A 4; GS C 6, N 4; GSF A 11 (as the last trait in a series of five, this trait is out of place), †C 6, J 4. In FF A 7, B 9, the trait is assigned to the mother. In FF E 12 and 16 it is assigned to both mother and sister, while the wife has disappeared completely. This confusion arises from the fact that FF A and B provide for all possible members of the immediate family. This situation

> GE B 6 And what wul ye leive to your bairns and your wife?
> The warldis room, late them beg thrae life.[1]

As we have seen, tradition corrupts the murderer's self-inflicted punishment, exposure in an open boat, into exile and hence, by a ready development, the wife joins the husband in exile in both English and Swedish texts.[2] No significance attaches to the agreement in detail, since the agreement has arisen independently by the operation of forces always present in oral transmission. In texts (from Finland only) in which the wife is given permission to marry again we have evidently a corruption,[3] for in them the children are expected to weep.

The exact form of the original trait is difficult to determine. Of course we have only to select between leaving the wife in grief and telling her to earn her livelihood by spinning. The second trait is well established in Northern tradition, which may and probably did preserve the old form. Its complete absence in English tradition is, however, somewhat disquieting. Conceivably grief, being so natural and elemental, represents a weakened, generalized form, which can arise spontaneously. On the other hand, grief is a trait which is very widely distributed, being found in Finnish, Finnish Swedish, Swedish, and English tradi-

---

is clearly an expansion of recent origin. Parallel expansion is particularly obvious in the case of the father who is assigned the task of spinning nets, e.g.:

> FF B 8 "Minne heität taattosi vanhan?
> Mieron verkkoja paikatkohon."
>
> Where do you leave your father?
> He may knit nets.

The development of this trait from the wife's (mother's) spinning is apparent.

[1] So also in GS E 5. There is little likelihood of any direct relationship between English and Swedish tradition in this case.

[2] GE I 14, J 6, N 7, O 5, P 6, Q 4, R 4, T 6; GS M 6. See also remarks above, p. 28.

[3] FF A 8, B 10; GSF B 8.

tion. We might therefore argue that spinning is a speciali-
zation. In this situation the oldest text, GS A of the seven-
teenth century, might be expected to cast a deciding vote,
if we had access to it. Certainly no trait other than these
two deserves consideration for a moment.

Children.—Quite naturally the children are left to beg or
to be cared for by friends.[1] We need not perhaps distinguish too sharply between these two traits. At first sight
it seems that English tradition knows nothing of leaving
the children to the care of friends, but in many texts the
trait appears in the assignment of the children to the
grandmother's care, e.g.:

> GE L 15 And what will ye do wi your wee son?
>   I'll leave him wi you, my dear mother,
>   To keep in remembrance of me.
>
>   16 What will ye do wi your houses and lands?
>   I'll leave them wi you, my dear mother,
>   To keep my own babie.[2]

In these texts, it will be noticed, the wife joins her husband
in exile. It is consequently possible and even probable that
the original disposition of the children, at least in these
texts, was leaving them in their mother's care. When the
mother joined her husband in exile, the children were
simply transferred to the grandmother. The combination
of the children's fate with the disposition of the property is
discussed later. In Finnish tradition the trait displays a
curious expansion, which is of recent origin, e.g.:

> FF A 9 Mihinkäs nuoren pojkais heität?
>   Käykään koulua, kärsikään wihtoja.

---

[1] In the following texts we have begging: GD A 5; GE A 11 (*old son*), B 6 (*wife
and children*); GS C 7, E 5 (*wife and children*), D 8, F 8, N 5; GSF A 10, †B9, C 5,
D 5. On a special development in English tradition see the next note. The
elaborate inventions of Finnish tradition are discussed later.

[2] See also GE J 7 (*three babes*), O 3 (*children*), †P 4–5, †Q 5–6, R 5, and the
remarks below. GE T 7 is distorted by parallelism.

10 Minnekkäs sai nuoren poikais heität?
   Kaykään metsässä, syötään marjoja,
   Elköön ikänään mina toiwokoo.

Where do you leave your young son?
He may go to school, suffer the rod there.

Where do you leave your young daughter?
She may go to the forest, eat berries,
I do not wish to see [her].[1]

This expansion in which special duties are assigned to a son and a daughter arises from a desire to provide for every member of the family. It bears no evidence of being an old trait, although a similar expansion is found in Virginian tradition.[2]

On the whole it seems most probable that the children were left in the care of the wife or friends; the distinction between that disposition of them and leaving them to beg is so evanescent and so likely to shift in one direction or the other that a decision is impossible. Again the old Swedish text (GS A) might settle the matter for us.

Property.—The murderer leaves behind his property to neglect and ruin, e.g.:

GE B 5 And what wul ye doe wi your towirs and your ha,
   That were sae fair to see O?
   Ile let thame stand tul they down fa.

A corruption, to which we have already alluded, is seen in

GE I 16 What will ye do wi your houses and lands?
   I'll leave them wi you, my dear mother,
   To keep my own babie.

and in a slightly different form in

GE N 6 What will you do with your pretty little house and lot?
   Give it to my good old father
   To bring up my children for me.

[1] I follow Schröter's translation, although it is not entirely clear to me. Similar details are found in FF B 11, 12.

[2] See GE P 4–5, Q 5–6.

In certain American texts this passage is considerably altered, e.g.:

GE J 8 O what will you do with your house and land?
   I'll leave it here in care of you
   For to set my children free.[1]

Presumably we may see in this an echo of the redemption of slaves, although I have not been fortunate enough to find a particular song of which this passage might be a reminiscence.

The Swedish texts exhibit very interesting variations and new developments. Here the agricultural knowledge of the singers leads them to assign particularly appropriate forms of neglect for both fields and animals, e.g.:

GS D 9 Hvad skall du göra af kreaturen?
   Dem släpper jag på sjelfföda.

   10 Hvad skall du göra af åker och äng?
   Dem lägger för fäfot.[2]

and in a still more complete form:

GSF A 7 Vad skall du göra av åker och äng?
   De måste ju ligga för var mans fe.

   8 Vad skall du göra av kreaturen din?
   De måste ju ocksa stickas ihjäl.

   9 Vad skall du göra av din hus och knut?
   Di får ju väl ruttna knut från knut.[3]

or

GSF B 10 Vad skall du göra av din åker och äng?
   De måste falla under fäfot.

   11 Vad skall du göra utav din' hus?
   De måste rottna knut för knut.

   12 Vad skall du göra av din' penningar?
   Dem giver jag åt vänner och grannar.

[1] See also GE O 4.   [2] See also GS F 9, 10.

[3] We see *knut* has found its way into the first line of the stanza.

In view of these passages we may reasonably suppose that those Swedish texts in which only the house[1] or only the field[2] is mentioned are corrupt.

The tenacity with which tradition clings to this trait of the property is instructive and shows that the trait belongs to the original form of the ballad, although it has suffered greatly in the course of oral transmission. An exact reconstruction of the original form is probably out of the question, but we may, without much hesitation, reject the full Swedish forms as late expansions.

Other persons.—The sporadic occurrence of father, mother, brother, sister, and of even a dog in the ballad texts bears witness to the ease with which the parallel structure of the bequests lends itself to expansions. No old trait is found in these details. A survey of the evidence makes quite clear how these enlargements came about. The father is mentioned in various activities, e.g.:

> FF A 6 Minnekkäs wanhan isäis heitat?
> Käykään metsässä, hakatkaan halkoja.
>
> What do you leave your old father?
> He may go to the forest, cut wood there.

is clearly related to

> GSF B 6 Vad skall du göra utav din gamla fader?
> Han måste föda sig med yxen.[3]

This variation appears to be an invention of Finnish-Swedish singers. In FF B the father is told to knit nets—an act which is set in parallel with the spinning of the murderer's wife. The brother and sister of FF E result from a similar expansion by the force of parallelism. The murderer's mother often takes over the function of the

[1] GSF D 6.

[2] GS E 16; GSF J 6.   [3] See also FF E 10.

wife.[1] Finally, we have the dog as the murderer's companion:

> GSF C 7 Vad skall du göra med din trogna hund?
> Honom jag tager med på vandringen min.[2]

In all these variations we observe the desire to account for every member of the household. Inasmuch as mother as interlocutor, wife and children as objects of bequests, and brother as victim of the murder all find necessary places in the story, the temptation to bring in the father and even brother and sister is constantly present. The father is also introduced in English tradition, but in quite a different way, e.g.:

> GE J 5 Oh what will you tell your father dear
> When he comes home from town?[3]

or

> GE L 4 What will you do when your father comes home?
> I'll get aboard of yonder ship
> And sail away to sea.

The presence of the father in English tradition is late and unoriginal.

Table I on the opposite page shows the order in which the bequests are made, revealing no striking or important variations in details. The normal arrangement is W, C, P, which is no doubt original. We see once more that Percy's text (GE B) is disordered and stands apart from all other versions. It cannot possibly be the source of English traditional versions. Those English texts (chiefly American) in which the murderer's departure has become flight often transfer the wife to the last position, where, however, she

---

[1] She spins in FF A 7, B 9, E 12; GSF B 7, and weeps in GS M 8 (cf. the weeping of the children in GSF B 9).

[2] See the child in GE T 7.

[3] See further GE K 1, L 4, N 5, O 2. I need not distinguish the two types here exemplified.

TABLE I

ORDER OF BEQUESTS*

FF A	FF B	FF C	FF E	GD A	GE A	GE B	GE I	GE J
Father Mother W C 1} † C 2} †	Father Mother W C 1} † C 2} †	W	Father Mother Brother Sister	W C	W C Mother's curse	P W+C Mother's curse	W C P	W C P

GE K	GE L	GE N	GE O	GE P	GE Q	GE R
[Father]†	[Father]†	[Father]† P W†	[Father]† C P W†	C 1 C 2} W	W C 1 C 2}	W C

GE S	GE T	GS C	GS D	GS E	GS F	GS M	GS N
[Father]†	[Father]† W C	W C	W C P 1} † P 2}	W+C Paraphrases P†	W C P 1} † P 2}	W Mother	W C

GSF A	GSF B	GSF C	GSF D	GSF J
P 1} P 2} † P 3} C W	{Father Mother W C P 1} P 2} † P 3}	C W Dog	C P	W C P

*W = Wife; C = Children; P = Property. Those texts which omit the bequests are of course absent. The details of each variation from the normal may be found in the preceding tabulations and discussions or in the texts themselves below.

† The obelus indicates corruption.

does not receive a bequest but goes off with her husband never to return. This change is natural because she cannot receive a bequest, and also provides a satisfactory climax. The other texts in which W does not stand in the first place are disordered: GSF A and C have suffered serious damage and GSF D appears to have dropped the trait W. The persistence of the traits W, C, P, and the rigidity of their order in both English and Swedish tradition argues strongly in favor of their presence in the original form of the ballad. It is noteworthy that the trait of the mother's curse, which concludes GE A and GE B, is quite inconsistent with the traits W, C, P. Hence we are inclined to look on it with suspicion.

The curse which the son lays on the mother

> GE A 12 What wilt thou leave to thy mother dear,
> Son Davie, son Davie?
> A fire o coals to burn her, wi hearty cheer,
> And she'll never get mair o me.

makes so striking a close that the reader is inclined to keep it at any cost. Yet there can be no reasonable doubt, in my opinion, that we must surrender it as a contamination. Although we have threescore texts of the ballad, the trait is known in only GE A and B. Its infrequent occurrence is of course an argument of minor value, if taken alone; but we are not compelled to rest the case at this point. The trait's instability in the "Edward" ballads contrasts with its frequency in other ballads, e.g., "The Twa Brothers" (Child No. 11) and "Lord Randal" (Child No. 12), that is to say, in ballads of the same peculiar dialogue form. The trait cannot belong indiscriminately to all these ballads; one ballad must have borrowed from another,[1] although the borrowing may have taken place so long ago that we can no longer identify borrower and lender. For the pres-

---

[1] We need not determine now what the interrelations are, although the problem is attractive and seemingly not insoluble.

ent argument we shall be content if we can find reasons for believing that the trait cannot have belonged to "Edward" from the first. The trait's instability, its non-appearance in the Scandinavian versions (which appear to have branched off from the main stem rather early), as well as the absence of any significant connection between trait and story awaken our suspicions. Furthermore, this ill wish for the mother is firmly established in "Lord Randal,"[1] and may have spread from that ballad to others.[2] Inasmuch as the trait frequently appears along with the nuncupative will and inasmuch as the declining vigor of the "Edward" tradition makes easier the absorption of new and foreign elements, the presence of this trait in GE A and B may be explained as arising by contamination. We are encouraged in this belief by observing that the insertion of the curse brings disorder into the series of bequests: in GE A no mention is made of the property and in GE B the sequence is clumsily arranged. We cannot for a moment concede that the sequence in GE A is original and that no disposition was made of the property. In GE B, which is fifty years older, the property is mentioned, and it appears in both the American tradition, which has presumably maintained an independent existence for several generations, and the Scandinavian tradition, which is equally old and distinct. The fields of GS D are reminiscences of the estate of the English ballad; see, e.g.:

> GS D 10 Hvad skall du göra af åker och äng?
> Den lägger för fäfot.[3]

A trait so widely known, so old—it is as old as any detail in the present form of the "Edward" ballads—and so logically

---

[1] We have it in Italian, English, Swedish, and German versions and elsewhere; see Child I 152 ff.

[2] See *ibid.* 143.

[3] See also GS E 16, F 10. In general, Scandinavian tradition lacks the trait.

39

and necessarily a part of the story cannot be discarded. Nor need we stop here. The form in GE A is explicable as a contamination from an obvious source. A stronger case for the rejection of a trait can scarcely be made out.[1]

In the next set of comparisons we are able to make a point which is theoretically and practically of the highest interest and importance. It has been assumed that incidents have originally a place in one particular narrative and that they have entered other tales by the process of contamination. The significance of the assumption in determining our ideas regarding the earliest state of primitive narrative is obvious. We must not imagine incidents and episodes floating about in a vacuum awaiting a chance to attach themselves to a story. From the very beginning incidents were definitely associated with narratives and were not at any time free molecules to be combined in an atomic structure of a story. Of course this assumption, which is Aarne's,[2] has been attacked and even violently attacked. But no one has looked to see what the facts were, instead of talking in metaphysical terms. In the present instance we have a trait which has never been carefully studied; the circumlocutions for "never" in folk song have been thrown together indiscriminately.[3] If we examine the mass more

---

[1] A further reason for the rejection of the curse appears below in the discussion of the paraphrases for "never."

[2] *FF Communications* XIII 11.

[3] The paraphrases offer food for thought and deserve examination for their own sake. Some of the comparisons are old and traditional; some are derived from ancient riddling lists of impossibilities; still others are definitely Christian in origin. See the long note in Child I 437 and Böckel *Psychologie der Volksdichtung*[2], 199. Very interesting in this connection is the extract from a Västergötland wedding song which my friend Dr. Sverker Ek calls to my attention:

> "At Swanen förr matte siunka til Grund
> och Stenen på Watnena flyta,
> Än någon Olust thet Kärleeks Förbund
> Mått' hindra och Sämjona bryta."

[Footnote continued on following page]

closely, we find that certain paraphrases are widely used, while others are narrowly restricted to certain contexts. In "Edward" and "Sven i Rosengård" both types of paraphrases are commingled. Our critical examination of these ballads leads us to believe that their present state is due to contamination. One paraphrase, which is found only in these two ballads, is particularly apposite, and we are justified in concluding that it belongs to these two ballads alone. Another paraphrase, which appears frequently in these ballads, proves on closer study to be utterly incongruous, and we therefore conclude that it has entered the ballads as a contamination. We have here the two possible situations: one trait is discovered to be peculiar to a single narrative and another trait, which is widely known, has been shown to be an interloper. Of course the first instance provides a direct illustration of the truth of the assumption and no particular interest attaches to it, inasmuch as no one has doubted that the assumption was true, at least of certain traits. The second instance shows that we can take the various combinations in which a widely known trait occurs and by processes of "higher criticism" eliminate one of these combinations as secondary in origin. This "higher criticism" employs the principles of the historico-geographical method. We can imagine eliminating in similar fashion all but one of the combinations in which the trait occurs and arriving by this means at a single primitive combination (or story) from which all the others radiate. On this occasion we shall take only the first step in the series of eliminations and consequently only the first step toward demonstrating Aarne's assump-

---

Taken from *Brollopsskrift tillägnad Kanutius Bäfwerfält* (1652), in Joh. Götlind *En Västgötabok* (Sala 1919) 55 in Erik Neuman's chapter "Nagra mer eller mindre västgötska bröllopsdikter." The existence of this parallel to the paraphrases is of course not convincing evidence that "Sven i Rosengård" was the source.

tion. All the other steps are exactly the same as this first one, and I am inclined to believe that in general no insuperable obstacles will present themselves in going on to the ultimate conclusion. Of course, it is conceivable—and in many cases, not improbable—that we may ultimately arrive at an *impasse* where the trait seems equally appropriate to several themes and equally attached to them all. In this case we have a situation which does not in itself disprove Aarne's assumption, for we must now turn our attention from the individual trait to the themes as units. It may be possible to show that the several themes are of very different ages and in this way attain to a definite conclusion. At the worst, we must content ourselves with a *non liquet*. Certainly nothing in all this speaks for the notion of episodes as free agents seeking tales to which to attach themselves.

The nuncupative will must be original. Such a will is a logical consequence of the situation and follows directly from what we have learned about the bottomless boat. Only death makes the murderer's exile irrevocable and justifies him in declaring his final wishes. We come now to the consideration of the paraphrases for "never" which so often form the ballad's termination. From the tabulation which follows it appears that the paraphrases properly end with an allusion to the Day of Judgment. In short, the murderer acknowledges his crime and realizes that his punishment endures while this world lasts. It is therefore more than probable that some hint of this situation existed in the original ballad, but tradition has long since forgotten the meaning of the hint and has fallen upon evil ways by developing it into interminable folly. The tabulation is as follows:

LIST OF PARAPHRASES FOR "NEVER"*

(1) Naar alle Kvinder bliver Enke. (var. När kyrkan blifver enka); (2) Naar alle Mænd bliver døde; (3) Naar Huse og Gaarde bliver øde; (4) Naar vi ser hvide Ravne; (5) Naar vi ser sorte Svaner; (6) Naar vi ser Fjedern synke; (7) Naar vi ser Stenen flyde; (8) Naar vi ser Havet brænde; (9) Naar alle piger bliver giftede; (10) När alla enbär mogna; (11) Naar vi ser Verdens Ende (variant forms are included); (12) När der är inga bänkar; (13) När tallen löfgas; (14) När björken han barras; (15) När stjärnorna dansa på himlen blå; (16) När ålla klockor klämta; (17) När dagarna ända; (18) När verlden blir till intet; (19) När solen går upp vestan; (20) När solen går ned östan.

	GD A	B	GN	GS A‡	B	C	D	E	F	G	H	J	K	L	M	N
1	7	7	19	4	5	4	†1	4	-	5	13	14	17	16		4
2	6	6	8	7	4	5	12	5		4	†14	7	18		7	5
3	9	4				7	7	6	7	6	7	6	11	19		7
4	19	11		11		6	†7	6		7	6	5		20		
5							10	4	10	11			5	4		
6							9	5	9		4					
7							†1	10	†1							
8							11	9	11							
11							13									
							14									

GS F A	B	C	D	E	F	G	H	J	FF A	B	C	D	E
4	14	15	4	7	5	-	13	5	19	4	-	-	4
5	†13	7	†15	†13	4		14	4	7	†5			
6	4	4+5	11	14	7		4	7	6	7			
7	5	†20		9			5	19	11	6			
11	6	†16	11				9			†19			
	7	†11					11			15			
	11									11			

*For convenience I give the paraphrases in the original languages, inasmuch as some are corruptions. I have not attempted to set the corruptions in order. Forms marked with a star are discussed later. The close relation of 1, 2, 9, and 10 is obvious; apparently 9 has arisen out of 1 by contrast.

† The obelus indicates corruptions.

‡ I take these details, which are all we know of the text of GS A, from Olrik's notes in *Danmarks gamle Folkeviser* VI 144. The order and number of paraphrases for "never" is uncertain. To those given in this tabulation we must add "Naar Ilden bliver vaad" and "Naar Stenen staar i Blomme."

At this point a brief critical examination will prove very helpful. Child[1] listed a number of typical paraphrases for "never" and collected a large number of instances unfortunately without classifying them. On examining these instances more closely we find them falling into two large groups; those which belong to lists of mere impossibilities[2] and those which have some more definite meaning and appropriateness. The distinction need not be sharply made or insisted upon in any particular case, but in the following paraphrases, for example, we see at once an obvious interpretation in the light of Christian story and belief:

> Naar alle Kvinder bliver Enke (1)
> Naar alle Mænd bliver døde (2)
> Naar Huse og Gaarde bliver øde (3)
> Naar vi ser Havet brænde (8)
> När stjärnorna dansar på himlen blå (15)
> När alla klockor klämta (16).

The interpretation is summed up in

> När dagarna ända (17)
> När verlden blir till intet (18).

It is exactly these paraphrases which are most firmly associated with our ballad; both English and Swedish tradition employ them with relative intelligence. Just these paraphrases, moreover, are found in GS A, the ballad text of 1690. Consequently their association with the ballad is as ancient as anything we know about the ballad. They are not commonplaces for every ballad-singer to twist to his whim, but are, on the contrary, the property of "Edward" and "Sven i Rosengård."

Many paraphrases in the second group are found in other contexts or are apparently nonce inventions, created casually by a singer to express an impossibility, e.g.:

[1] *English and Scottish Popular Ballads* I 437.

[2] It is, to be sure, often feasible for us to distinguish relative age in these; see the remarks below.

Naar vi ser hvide Ravne (4)
Naar vi ser sorte Svaner (5)
Naar vi ser Fjedern synke (6)
Naar vi ser Stenen flyde (7)
När tallen löfgas (13)
När björken han barras (14).

Precisely these paraphrases enter and leave our texts at will. The similarity to the first group is, although superficial, so obvious that attraction takes place and the ballad grows by accretion of members from the second group. Such accretion is all the more likely when the full force of the paraphrases in the first group with their allusion to the Day of Judgment has been obscured or forgotten. We are of course chiefly concerned with the relative ages of the two combinations of ballad and paraphrase and not with the absolute age of the paraphrases alone. It should be quite clear that the ballad's union with the first group of paraphrases is much older than its union with the second; in fact, that the original ballad almost certainly contained something resembling the first group of paraphrases. Yet we need scarcely point out that many paraphrases in the second group (e.g., the comparison with white ravens, sinking feathers) are very ancient indeed and possibly existed before our ballad. Others are quite as certainly recent invention, e.g.:

Wenns schneiet rothe Rosen,
wenns regnet kühlen Wein,
so lang sollst du mein harren.[1]

Even the oldest of such paraphrases—and some of them certainly existed before "Edward" came into being—cannot have been part of the original ballad.

This tabulation of the paraphrases for "never" makes clear several facts about their development and the

[1] Reifferscheid *Westfälische Volkslieder* (1879) 23 No. 11 stanza 3. Practically all the German paraphrases cited by Child are variants of this theme.

45

changes which have occurred in them. It will be noticed, for example, that incidents 13 and 14, which are obviously inventions belonging to Sweden or Finland, have not yet firmly established themselves in the ballad. No particular significance attaches to the versions in which this pair of incidents is found; such conventional phrases creep into the list at any time and consequently they cannot be used by themselves to prove relationships.[1] The tenacity with which incidents 4, 5, 6, 7, cling together is worthy of mention and is comparable to the pair 10 and 11, which seem to occur ordinarily in combination. Only the group 4, 5, 6, 7 or some part of it might lay claim to a place in the ballad, and this combination as well as the individual members is old and hackneyed. Olrik suggests[2] that "Svend Vonved" has borrowed from our ballad. The passage in question is as follows:

> Nar maa ieg lade blande vin?
> nar maa ieg venthe komme din?
>
> Naar stennen tager thill at flyde,
> och raffnen begynnther at huidtnne.
>
> Och aller flyder stiennen,
> och aller huidner raffnen.
>
> Aller flydder stienen,
> och aller thør y mig venthe mehr.[3]

These comparisons are not peculiarly characteristic of "Edward" and have been traced back to Kormak the Scald in the tenth century.[4] Since we find nothing similar in the English texts of "Edward" we conclude that these

---

[1] I cannot see that GS E, J, K; GSF B, E, H are more nearly related to one another and certainly the possession of all or part of the pair of incidents is slight evidence.

[2] *Danmarks gamle Folkeviser* VI 144.

[3] *Danmarks gamle Folkeviser* I 240.

[4] Bugge *Aarbøger f. nord. Oldk.* 2. række IV (1889) 6 f.

comparisons, i.e., incidents 4, 5, 6, 7, have been added to the ballad in Scandinavia.

The English ballads often end with a comparatively brief allusion to the impossibility of the sun and moon dancing on the green.[1] Some traces of a similar allusion are found in the North, e.g.:

> GD B 4 Hvornaar bliver alle Piger giftede?
> Naar Solen den staar norden op.

or

> GSF J 10 När börjar stenen flyta?
> När solen går upp i väster.

or

> GS M 13 När går sol upp vestan?
> När hon går ned östan.
>
> 14 När går sol ned östan,
> Du Sven i Rosengård?
> Aldrig före Dome-dagen,
> Kära moder min,
> Ni vänten mig sent, men jag kommer aldrig.

The picture is clearly occupied with details from the Last Judgment. And in the following versions the outlines are even more clearly drawn:

> GSF C 12 Och när svartnar solen?
> När himlens klockor klämta.
>
> 13 När klämta himlens klockor?
> När domsbasunen klingar.

and

> GSF D 8 När ljusnar svarta korpen?
> När stjärnan faller till jorden.
>
> 9 När faller stjärnan till jorden?
> När domens dagar stunda.

---

[1] See Nos. 15, 19, and 20 in the tabulation, and the remarks below.

With this scene in mind we see more significance in some of
the details, e.g., incidents 1, 2, 3, 8, 15, 16, 17, 18, 19, 20,
which give evidence that the singer had still some notion
of the Last Judgment as the background of these paraphrases. In many texts these portents explicitly signify the
end of the world, e.g.:

> GD A 14 Naar ser vi Havet brænde?
>   Naar vi ser Verdens Ende;
>
> GS D 18 När blir kyrkan enka?
>   Jo, innan verldens ända;[1]
>
> GS H 8 När flyter stenen?
>   När som domen kommer;[2]
>
> GSF E 9 När bliver alla flicker gifta?
>   Uppå den stora domedagen.
>
>   10 När kommer den stora domedagen?
>   Uppå den yttersta dagen.[3]

Those versions which conclude with the bald assertion that
these impossibilities will never be, preserve a last weak
trace of the old concept, e.g.:

> GN 8 Naar kvitnar raven?
>   Det sker dog aldrig;

and

> GS C 11 Och när flyter gråsten?
>   Stenen flyter aldrig.[4]

The ultimate stage of degeneration is of course the failure
to mention the Last Judgment or any paraphrase which
has finality.[5] Few singers wish to develop the notion of the
Last Judgment, but an example of this is seen in

> GS L 4 När kommer du igen då?
>   När dagarne få ända.

---

[1] See also GS F 18.

[2] See also GSF A 16, B 19.   [3] See also GSF H 11.

[4] See also GS N 9 and the refrain "Ni vänten mig sent eller aldrig."

[5] See GS E, J, K; GSF F.

5 När få dagarne ända?
   När verlden blir till intet.

6 När blir verlden till intet?
   När vi skall fram för domen.

7 Hvad får du i domen?
   Förbannelse och mörker.

On the basis of this evidence we conclude that the Scandinavian ballad originally ended with an allusion to the Judgment Day, an allusion readily grasped because of its pictorial quality. This pictorial quality led in the course of oral transmission to the manifold substitutions and contaminations seen in the tabulation. For the moment, we shall not venture to specify which one of these paraphrases was original. Comparison may determine that fact for us. An endeavor to find a basis for comparison brings forth some surprising evidence. The oldest, uncontaminated English texts of "Edward" and many modern ones know nothing of these concluding paraphrases,[1] but the weight of the evidence proves to be slight. At first we might suspect this to be the primitive form of the ballad, to which the paraphrases were later added. Inasmuch as paraphrases are found in England and America as well as in Scandinavia, such a deduction is not, however, well founded. And the conviction that some paraphrase existed in the primitive ballad is supported by the similarities between English and Scandinavian tradition. In the contaminated English texts and in modern traditional English and American versions we find a single type of paraphrase, which varies greatly in details, e.g.:

GE D 20 Whan the sun and moon dances on the green,
         And that will never be;[2]

[1] GE A, B, |C, G, J, †K, N, †U.

[2] GE E 17 (*leap on yon hill*), F 24 (*gae three times round*), H 12.

49

GE I 17 When the sun and the mune meet on yon hill,
    And I hope that'll never be;[1]

or

GE M 8 When the sun sets into yanders sycamore tree,
    And it's that will never be.

The general similarity between the English forms and the previously cited Scandinavian paraphrases is obvious, and it is convincing proof that we are dealing with the original ending of the ballad. As we have seen, the Scandinavian paraphrases deal with the Last Judgment and are therefore involved with Christian eschatology. The notion of the sun dancing on the green which we find in "Edward" is not readily explained. It is certainly associated with English and Scandinavian superstitions about the sun dancing on Easter morning, and in the absence of an explanation from Christian story these may have a heathen origin.[2] In any event, the allusion is designed to emphasize the finality of the murderer's fate. The consciousness that we are dealing with irrevocable acts and with circumstances which endure to the end of the world is, furthermore, made clear in the Scandinavian refrain:

Ni vänten mig sent, men jag kommer aldrig

and the parallels to it in English tradition; e.g.:

GE A 9 And ye'll never see mair o me.[3]

The constant presence of some such phrase implying "never" leads us to suppose that we are dealing with a reminiscence of something lost, and the tenacity with which tradition clings to it—the phrase occurs in the great

[1] GE O 6, P 7, Q 7, R 6, S 4, T 9.

[2] See E. A. Philippson *Germanisches Heidentum bei den Angelsachsen* ("Kölner anglistische Arbeiten" IV [1929]) 109–10.

[3] For comment on the development of the refrain see the remarks below.

majority of English texts[1]—makes us certain that such a supposition is correct. An important consequence of this deduction is that the paraphrases for "never" belong to the story. In no instance do they occur in combination with the son's curse (GE A, B). The paraphrases for "never" and the curse are incompatible. Since we have accepted the paraphrases as original, we must reject the curse. It is important to observe that we have already reached this conclusion by a different route.[2]

We may now examine the various refrains, by way of completing the critical study of the ballad. It is clear on tabulation that the original refrain concerned mother or son or perhaps both in some parallel structure. The agreement of Finnish, Scandinavian, and English tradition on this point is convincing evidence. We cannot readily determine the exact form of the refrain, but its main outlines are clear enough. The English versions do not give much information. Compare

> GE A 1 What bluid's that on thy coat lap,
> *Son Davie, son Davie?*
> What bluid's that on thy coat lap?
> *And the truth come tell to me.*
>
> 2 It is the bluid of my great hawk,
> *Mother lady, mother lady;*
> It is the bluid of my great hawk,
> *And the truth I have told to thee.*

and

> GE B 1 Why dois your brand sae drap wi bluid,
> *Edward, Edward,*
> Why dois your brand sae drap wi bluid,
> And why sae sad gang yee O?

---

[1] It is found in 13 of the 21 versions. Of the 8 versions in which it does not occur, 3 are fragments (GE C, K, U) and 2 are contaminated (GE G). The rather imperfectly preserved American texts GE J, N lack the phrase. Only GE A and B, which are discussed in the text, appear to be important.

[2] See above, p. 38.

51

> O I hae killed my hauke sae guid,
> *Mither, mither,*
> O I hae killed my hauke sae guid,
> And I had nae mair bot hee O.

Elsewhere in the English tradition we have little or no trace of the parallelism of mother and son in the refrain. The late American tradition, which follows a tradition already firmly established in Scotland, is clearly related to GE A and its type, although degeneration has set in, e.g.:

> GE J 1 How come that blood on your shirt sleeve?
> *Pray, son, now tell to me.*
> It is the blood of the old grey mare
> That ploughed that corn for me.[1]

The situation is necessarily much obscured in the contaminated texts where the refrain does not readily accord with the theme of the second ballad, but even here there are sufficient traces of the refrain last mentioned.

The refrain which contains mother and son in parallel is most clearly seen in the Finnish

> FF B 1 Mistäs tulet, kustas tulet,
> *Poikani iloinen?*
> Meren rannalta, meren rannalta,
> *Äitini kultainen.*
>
> Whence do you come, whence do you come,
> *My happy son?*
> From the shore of the sea, from the shore of the sea,
> *My gold mother.*[2]

and the Finnish tradition generally. In the Scandinavian tradition a similar form appears with sufficient frequency[3] to justify us in connecting it with the Finnish form and therefore in regarding it as old, e.g.:

---

[1] A similar refrain is generally found in the American tradition; see, e.g., GE G, K, M, N, O, P, Q, R, S, T. It is found also in English tradition; see GE D 16, 19, 20; E 12 ff.; I 10 ff., and the disordered forms in GE F, H.

[2] A term of endearment.

[3] GD B; GS N; GSF B, C, D, †E, †F, †H; FF A, B, C, D.

GD B 1 Hvornaar mon jeg dig vente?
Svend i Rosenslund!
Naar Stenene de flyder,
Min hjærtens-kære Mor!

and

GS N 1 A var har du varit, *ja Sven i Rosengård?*
Jo jag har vattnat fålarna, *ja kära moder vår.*

Ordinarily we have in Scandinavia a combined refrain, in which the line

Ni vänten mig sent, men jag kommer aldrig!

has been added to the preceding simpler type of refrain.[1] I suspect that we have here a line which was not originally a refrain, but which has become one in the process of transmission. Parallels to this line exist in the English ballads, e.g.:

GE A 9 And ye'll never see mair o me;

B 5 For here never mair maun I bee O;

D 20 And that will never be.[2]

We can see the gradual development of this line in the direction of a refrain in the following series of stanzas:

GE A 9 I'll set my foot in a bottomless ship,
Mother lady, mother lady:
I'll set my foot in a bottomless ship
And ye'll never see mair o me.

10 What wilt thou leave to thy poor wife,
Son Davie, son Davie?
Grief and sorrow all her life,
And she'll never see mair o me.

11 What wilt thou leave to thy old son,
Son Davie, son Davie?
I'll leave him the weary world to wander up and down,
And he'll never get mair o me.

[1] GD A; GN; GS B, C, D, E, F, G, H, J, K, L, ?M; GSF A, C, G, J.

[2] See further GE E 17, 18; F 24; I 17; M 8; O 6.

53

12 What wilt thou leave to thy mother dear,
   Son Davie, son Davie?
A fire o coals to burn her, wi hearty cheer,
   And she'll never get mair o me.

The branching-off of the Scandinavian tradition occurred long before the rise of the modern corrupt oral versions of the English and American tradition, for the older form, represented by the compounded refrain, has persisted in Finnish and in some Scandinavian versions. The compounded refrain arose in Scandinavia by the action of the same forces that produced the corruption of the English ballad, but the developments in the two regions have been entirely independent. The predominance of the older form, i.e., the uncompounded refrain, both in the West (GN, Norway; GS N, Bohuslän) and in the Far East (Swedish and Finnish in Finland) indicates that the new form, i.e., the compounded refrain, which has arisen in the center, has not extended itself over the whole area. The older form is found on the periphery.

We can discern a few more facts regarding the ballad's dissemination beyond establishing its spread from England. Olrik observes that the ballad is known in Jutland, where most Danish ballads have been found sooner or later, and that the South Sælland form (GD A) displays Swedish syntactical peculiarities. The second Danish version is a fragment from Fyn. The chaotic preservation of the Danish ballad, its Swedish flavor, and the localization of the two versions not far from Swedish soil lead us to look to Sweden as the land of origin. The Norwegian version (GN) is almost pure Danish. Yet inasmuch as its first singer bears a name which might suggest Swedish antecedents, we might conceivably assign this ballad also to Sweden. The similarity of GN to the West Swedish version (GS N) from Bohuslän, the only version which has been recorded from Western Sweden, seems to indicate the existence of a West Swedish recension. If more Norwegian and West Swedish versions were at our command it might be possible to trace the ballad's path in this all-important region. The Finnish versions are obvious derivatives of Swedish sources and, as we have seen, have ventured upon alterations of their own.

Although this careful examination of the details brings us to a conclusion regarding the ballad's history and dissemination, we cannot but inquire whether our conclusion will be acceptable when seen in a longer perspective. The courtly background of the older English versions (Percy, Herd, Motherwell) implies customs and manners quite foreign to the world in which the modern traditional forms move: the murderer has a sword, a horse, and a hawk; he has property, even a towered hall, to dispose of; although he has children, he still lives with his mother;[1] and he suffers an ancient punishment. But in the modern tradition he is a farmer who curries or waters horses, quarrels meanly with his brother, gives thought to the farm animals he will leave behind, and takes refuge in cowardly flight. The theme is debased and vulgarized. Clearly the development can have been in but one direction: the older form has degenerated in the mouths of the modern ballad singers. This downward progress has taken place independently in Scandinavia and Great Britain. Since no trace of the ballad's earlier courtly form has been found in Scandinavia,[2] and since the ballad seems relatively well established in English tradition, we must conclude that it passed from Scotland or England to Scandinavia.

[1] This custom is medieval, although it persisted into recent times in the North; see Olrik in *Danmarks gamle Folkeviser* VI 143, 144.

[2] Probably no importance attaches to the mention of a possible French parallel to "Edward"; see Geijer and Afzelius II 80 n.

TEXTS

TEXTS

FF A

H. R. von Schröter *Finnische Runen, finnisch und deutsch* (Upsala 1819) 126–29 "Werinen poika; Der blutige Sohn"; reprinted with insignificant changes in the second edition (ed. G. H. von Schröter [Stuttgart 1834] 150–55); translated into Swedish in Arwidsson *Svenska fornsånger* (Stockholm 1837) II 88–89. I reprint the text of the first edition except for the refrain.

1   Mistäs tulet? mistas tulet?
      Minun Pojkain iloinen.
    Meren rannalt', meren rannalt',
      Muori kultasein.

2   Mitä sieltä tekemästä?
    Hewostani juottamasta.

3   Missäs jakkuis saween teit?
    Hewoinen tallais, hewoinen tallais.

4   Missäs miekkais wereen teit[?]
    Tapoin ainoan weljeni.

5   Minnekkäs siitten ite jouwut?
    Muille maille wierahille.

6   Minnekkäs wanhan isäis heität?
    Käykään metsässä, hakatkaan halkoja,
    Elköön ikänään minua toiwokoo.

7   Mihinkäs wanhan Muoriis heität?
    Istukaan nurkassa, watwokoon tappuroita,
    Elköön ikänään minua toiwokoo.

8   Mihinkäs nuoren pojkais heität?
      Käykään koulua, kärsikään wihtoja.

9   Minnekkäs sen nuoren piikais heität?
      Käykään metsässä, syötään marjoja,
      Elköön ikänään mina toiwokoo.

10   Millonkas sielta kotian tulet?
      Silloin kuin päiwä pohjasta paistaa.

11   Millonkas päiwä pohjasta paistaa?
      Silloin kuin kiwi wein päällä pyörii.

12   Millonkas kiwi wein päällä pyörii?
      Silloin kuin höyhen pohjaan painuu.

13   Millonkas höyhen pohjaan painuu?
      Silloin kuin kaikki Tuomiolle tuloo.

TRANSLATION

Whence do you come, whence do you come, my happy son? From the seashore, from the seashore, my gold mother (i.e., beloved mother). What did you there? I watered the horses. Why is your jacket stained with dirt? The horses kicked. How did your sword get so bloody? I killed my only brother. Where will you go now? Far into foreign lands. Where will you leave your old father? Let him go to the forest and cut wood there; may he never wish to see me again. Where will you leave your old mother? May she heckle flax; may she wish never to see me again. Where will you leave your young wife? Let her go about adorned and take another; may she wish never to see me again. Where will you leave your young son? May he go to school and suffer rods there. Where will you leave your young daughter? Let her go to the forest to eat berries; may she wish never to see me again. When will you come home again? When the sun rises in the north. When will the sun rise in the north? When stones dance on water. When will stones dance on water? When feathers sink to the bottom. When will feathers sink to the bottom? When all come to judgment.

FF B

E. Lönnrot *Kanteletar elikkä suomen kansan vanhoja lauluja ja virsiä*[5] ("Suomalaisen kirjallisuuden seuran toimituksia" III [Helsinki 1906]) x–xi No. 4 "Velisurmaaja."[1]

1   Mistäs tulet, kustas tulet,
       Poikani iloinen?
       Meren rannalta, meren rannalta,
       Äitini kultainen.[2]

2   Mitä sieltä tekemästä?
       Hevostani juottamasta.

3   Mist' on selkäsi saveen tullut?
       Hevonen huiskasi hännällänsä.

4   Mist' on jalkasi vereen tullut?
       Hevonen polkasi rauallansa.

5   Mist' on miekkasi vereen tullut?
       Pistin veljeni kuoliaksi.

6   Mintähen sinä veljesi pistit,
       Poikani poloinen?
       Mintähen naistani nauratteli,
       Muorini kultainen.

7   Minne nyt sinä itse jouvut?
       Muille maille vierahille.

---

[1] Lönnrot's manuscript, which is still preserved in the archives of the Suomalaisen Kirjallisuuden Seura, exhibits some variants of which no account is taken in the printed *Kanteletar*. These variants probably indicate that Lönnrot had a second text before him. I note that the refrain refers to "maiden" (*nuori*) and not to "mother" (*äiti*) and in stanza 8 the father may either knit nets or go begging, and the variant "go begging" is used of the mother in stanza 9 as well.

[2] This refrain is used until stanza 6, from which point on another refrain is used.

8 Minne heität taattosi vanhan?
  Mieron verkkoja paikatkohon.

9 Minne heität maammosi vanhan?
  Mieron rihmoja keträtköhön.

10 Minne heität naisesi nuoren?
  Mieron miehiä katselkohon.

11 Minne heität poikasi nuoren?
  Mieron koulua kärsiköhön.

12 Minne heität tyttösi nuoren?
  Mieron karjoja kaitsekohon.

13 Koskas sieltä kotihin käännyt?
  Konsa korppi valkenevi.

14 Koskas korppi valkenevi?
  Konsa hanhi mustenevi.

15 Koskas hanhi mustenevi?
  Konsa kivi veen päällä pyörii.

16 Koskas kivi veen päällä pyörii?
  Konsa höyhen pohjaan painuu.

17 Koskas höyhen pohjaan painuu?
  Konsa päivä syänyöllä paistaa.

18 Koskas päivä syänyöllä paistaa?
  Konsa kuuhut kuumasti polttaa.

19 Koskas kuuhut kuumasti polttaa?
  Konsa tähet taivaalla tanssii.

20 Koskas tähet taivaalla tanssii?
  Konsa kaikki tuomiolle tullaan.

Whence do you come, my merry son? From the seashore, my dear mother [*var. maiden*]. What have you done there?[1] I have watered my horse. Why is your back spotted with clay? The horse brushed me with its tail. Why is your foot bloody? The horse kicked me with its iron [shoes]. Why is your sword bloody? I stabbed my brother. Why did you stab your brother? Because he put my wife to shame. What is your purpose? To hide myself and flee. Where do you leave your father? [*var.* refrain: Oh, where indeed?] He may knit nets [*var.* go begging]. Where do you leave your mother? She may spin at the spinning-wheel [*var.* go begging]. Where do you leave your young wife? She may look at men [*var.* bewail me]. Where do you leave your young son? He may suffer in school [*var.* suffer the rod and visit the school]. Where do you leave your young daughter? She may watch the cattle. When will you come home? [*var.* refrain: Oh, when indeed?] When the raven becomes white. When will the raven become white? When the goose becomes black. When will the goose become black? When the stone rolls on the water. When will the stone roll on the water? When the feather sinks to the bottom. When will the feather sink to the bottom? When the sun shines at midnight. When will the sun shine at midnight? When the moon burns with burning heat. When will the moon burn with burning heat? When the stars dance in heaven. When will the stars dance in heaven? When all come to judgment.[2]

FF C

Collected in Kalvola, South Tavastland, from Adolfine Montin, aged thirty-four, by Professor Kaarle Krohn about 1884.

1   Mistäs tulet, kustas tulet,
       Poikani poloinen.

2   Meren rannalta.

[3]

4   Hevostani uittamasta.

5   Mistä miekkas on vereen tullut?

6   Hevonen potkasi.

---

1 The refrain is omitted henceforth; from stanza 6 on it is "my wretched son." A variant refrain for the mother's stanzas is noted in the text.

2 Schott's translation (*Acta comparationis litt. univ.* [Kolosvár 1880–81] IV 129) is unsatisfactory.

7	Mistä takkis on saveen tullut?
8	Hevonen huiskasi hännällänsä.
9	Miksi hän naistani nauratteli?
10	Menen muille maille vierahille.
11	Mihinkäs jätät vaimosi nuoren?
12	Mieron tietä kulkemahan.

TRANSLATION

Whence do you come, my wretched son? From the seashore. From swimming my horse. Why is your sword wet? The horse stamped. Why is your coat bespattered with clay? The horse swished its tail. Why did he seduce your wife? I shall go to foreign lands. What do you leave your wife? She may go begging.

FF D

Written down March 17, 1823, in Åbo by J. J. Pippingsköld (d. 1832). The manuscript is now preserved in the library of the University in Helsingfors (shelfmark D.IV.47). This text has been printed in *Kansanopiston laulukirja* (1909) 336–37 No. 290. For information regarding Pippingsköld see the excellent monograph by Otto Anderson (*Johan Josef Pippingsköld och musiklivet i Åbo, 1808–1827* [Helsingfors 1927]). I am greatly indebted to Professor Tarkiainen for information regarding this text.

FF E

Suomen kansan vanhat runot (Keksi-Inkerin) IV No. 2701. From
Moloskoritsa, Central Ingria.

1	Mist' tulet, kustas tulet,
	Poikaini iloinen?
[2]	is evidently lacking.
3	Mist saappaas savvee soit?
4	Maateitä myöte kulkeissain,
	Likka lintusein.
5	Mistäs miekkas verree teit?
6	Tapoin miehen, saatoin päähä.[1]
7	Mihinkäs luulet joutusasi?
8	Jourein maille vierahille.
9	Mihin jätät sie issäis?
10	Käyköön metsäss, hakatkoo halkii.
11	Mihin jätät äiti seisi?
12	Istukoo nurkassa, ratvokoo villa.
13	Mihin jätät veikko seisi?
14	Punokoo nuora, lyököö koiraa.
15	Mihin jätät siskoseisi?
16	Kehratköö rihmaa, kutokoo kankast.
17	Kensas tuolta peisi pääset?
18	Kensa korppi valkenoopi.

[1] This line is borrowed from another ballad; see Krohn "Kalevalastudien II:
Lemminkäinen" *FF Communications* LXVII 40.

Whence do you come, my happy son? Why are your boots dirty?
From wandering along the highway, my girl, my little bird.[1] Why is
your sword so bloody? I have killed a man, I have put my head in
danger. Where do you expect to go? I went to foreign lands. To what
do you leave your father? Let him wander in the forest, split billets of
wood. To what do you leave your mother? Let her sit in the corner,
knit [?] wool. To what do you leave your brother? Let him plait a rope,
beat a dog. To what do you leave your sister? Let her spin yarn, weave
goods. When will you come back? When the raven turns white.

GD A

S. Grundtvig *Danmarks gamle Folkeviser* (Copenhagen 1895) VI
144–45 No. 340A. Taken down in Sydsælland in 1844 and 1846.

1 Hvor har du været saa længe?
   Svend i Rosensgaard!
  Og jeg har været i Enge,
   kære Moder vor!
  I vente mig sent eller aldrig!

2 Hvorfor er dit Sværd saa blodigt?
  For jeg har dræbt min Broder.

3 Hvor vil du dig hen vende?
  Jeg vil af Landet rende.

4 Hvor vil du gøre af Hustruen din?
  Hun skal spinde for Føden sin

5 Hvor vil du gøre af Børnene dine?
  Jeg vil sætte dem til Vennerne mine.

6 Naar vil du dig hjem vende?
  Naar alle Kvinder bliver Enke.

7 Naar bliver alle Kvinder Enke?
  Naar alle Mænd bliver døde.

[1] A term of endearment.

8   Naar bliver alle Mænd døde?
       Naar Huse og Gaarde bliver øde.

9   Naar bliver Huse og Gaarde øde?
       Naar vi ser hvide Ravne.

10   Naar ser vi hvide Ravne?
       Naar vi ser sorte Svaner.

11   Naar ser vi sorte Svaner?
       Naar vi ser Fjedren synke.

12   Naar ser vi Fjedren synke?
       Naar vi ser Stenen flyde.

13   Naar ser vi Stenen flyde?
       Naar vi ser Havet brænde.

14   Naar ser vi Havet brænde?
       Naar vi ser Verdens Ende.

GD B

S. Grundtvig *Danmarks gamle Folkeviser* (Copenhagen 1895) VI 145
No. 340B. Taken down in Fyn before 1884.

1   Hvornaar mon jeg dig vente?
          Svend i Rosenslund!
       Naar Stenene de flyder,
          Min hjærtens-kære Mor!

2   Hvornaar saa flyder Stenene?
       Naar Fjerene de synker.

3   Hvornaar saa synker Fjerene?
       Naar alle Piger bliver giftede.

4   Hvornaar bliver alle Piger giftede?
       Naar Solen den staar norden op.

GE A

Motherwell *Minstrelsy Ancient and Modern* (1827) 339 (reprinted in Child *English and Scottish Popular Ballads* I 169 No. 13A).

1   What bluid's that on thy coat lap,
        Son Davie, son Davie?
    What bluid's that on thy coat lap?
        And the truth come tell to me.

2   It is the bluid of my great hawk,
        Mother lady, mother lady:
    It is the bluid of my great hawk,
        And the truth I have told to thee.

3   Hawk's bluid was neer sae red,
        Son Davie, son Davie:
    Hawk's bluid was neer sae red,
        And the truth come tell to me.

4   It is the bluid of my greyhound,
        Mother lady, mother lady:
    It is the bluid of my greyhound,
        And it wadna rin for me.

5   Hound's bluid was neer sae red,
        Son Davie, son Davie:
    Hound's bluid was neer sae red,
        And the truth come tell to me.

6   It is the blood o my brither John,
        Mother lady, mother lady:
    It is the bluid o my brither John,
        And the truth I have told to thee.

7   What about did the plea begin,
        Son Davie, son Davie?

It began about the cutting of a willow wand
That would never been a tree.

8   What death dost thou desire to die,
      Son Davie, son Davie?
    What death dost thou desire to die?
      And the truth come tell to me.

9   I'll set my foot in a bottomless ship,
      Mother lady, mother lady:
    I'll set my foot in a bottomless ship,
      And ye'll never see mair o me.

10   What wilt thou leave to thy poor wife,
      Son Davie, son Davie?
    Grief and sorrow all her life,
      And she'll never see mair o me.

11   What wilt thou leave to thy old son,
      Son Davie, son Davie?
    I'll leave him the weary world to wander
      up and down,
      And he'll never get mair o me.

12   What wilt thou leave to thy mother dear,
      Son Davie, son Davie?
    A fire o coals to burn her, wi hearty cheer,
      And she'll never get mair o me.

GE B

Percy *Reliques of Ancient English Poetry* I (1765) 53 (reprinted in Child *English and Scottish Popular Ballads* I 169–70 No. 13B).

1   Why dois your brand sae drap wi bluid,
      Edward, Edward,
    Why dois your brand sae drap wi bluid,
      And why sae sad gang yee O?

O I hae killed my hauke sae guid,
    Mither, mither,
O I hae killed my hauke sae guid,
    And I had nae mair bot hee O.

2   Your haukis bluid was nevir sae reid,
    Edward, Edward,
Your haukis bluid was nevir sae reid,
    My deir son I tell thee O.
O I hae killed my reid-roan steid,
    Mither, mither,
O I hae killed my reid-roan steid,
    That erst was sae fair and frie O.

3   Your steid was auld, and ye hae gat mair,
    Edward, Edward,
Your steid was auld, and ye hae gat mair,
    Sum other dule ye drie O.
O I hae killed my fadir deir,
    Mither, mither,
O I hae killed my fadir deir,
    Alas, and wae is mee O!

4   And whatten penance wul ye drie, for that,
    Edward, Edward,
And whatten penance will ye drie for that?
    My deir son, now tell me O.
Ile set my feit in yonder boat,
    Mither, mither,
Ile set my feit in yonder boat,
    And Ile fare ovir the sea O.

5   And what wul ye doe wi your towirs and your ha,
    Edward, Edward?

And what wul ye doe wi your towirs and your ha,
    That were sae fair to see O?
Ile let thame stand tul they doun fa,
    Mither, mither,
Ile let thame stand tul they doun fa,
    For her nevir maun I bee O.

6   And what wul ye leive to your bairns and your wife,
    Edward, Edward?
And what wul ye leive to your bairns and your wife,
    Whan ye gang ovir the sea O?
The warldis room, late them beg thrae life,
    Mither, mither,
The warldis room, late them beg thrae life,
    For thame nevir mair wul I see O.

7   And what wul ye leive to your ain mither deir,
    Edward, Edward?
And what wul ye leive to your ain mither deir?
    My deir son, now tell me O.
The curse of hell frae me sall ye beir,
    Mither, mither,
The curse of hell frae me sall ye beir,
    Sic counseils ye gave to me O.

GE C[1]

Child *English and Scottish Popular Ballads* I 170 No. 13C.

1   O what did the fray begin about?
    My son, come tell to me:
It began about the breaking o the bonny hazel wand,
    And a penny wad hae bought the tree.

[1] Thanks are due Houghton Mifflin Co. for permission to reprint this text.

71

GE D

Jamieson *Popular Ballads* I (1806) 59 (reprinted in Child *English and Scottish Popular Ballads* I 440–41 No. 49D "The Twa Brothers").[1]

16 But whaten bluid's that on your sword, Willie?
    Sweet Willie, tell to me;
O it is the bluid o my grey hounds,
    They wadna rin for me.

17 It's nae the bluid o your hounds, Willie,
    Their bluid was never so red;
But it is the bluid of my true-love,
    That ye hae slain indeed.

18 That fair may wept, that fair may mournd,
    That fair may mournd and pin'd:
When every lady looks for her love,
    I neer need look for mine.

19 O whaten a death will ye die, Willie?
    Now, Willie, tell to me;
Ye'll put me in a bottomless boat,
    And I'll gae sail the sea.

20 Whan will ye come hame again, Willie?
    Now, Willie, tell to me;
Whan the sun and moon dances on the green,
    And that will never be.

---

[1] The first fifteen stanzas belong to "The Twa Brothers," but the conclusion, except for stanza 18, has been taken from "Edward." Only the conclusion need be printed here.

GE E

Motherwell *Minstrelsy Ancient and Modern* (1827) 60 (reprinted in Child *English and Scottish Popular Ballads* I 441–42 No. 49E "The Twa Brothers").[1]

12   When he sat in his father's chair,
        He grew baith pale and wan:
    O what blude's that upon your brow?
        O dear son, tell to me;
    It is the blude o my gude gray steed,
        He wadna ride wi me.

13   O thy steed's blude was neer sae red,
        Nor eer sae dear to me:
    O what blude's this upon your cheek?
        O dear son, tell to me;
    It is the blude of my greyhound,
        He wadna hunt for me.

14   O thy hound's blude was neer sae red,
        Nor eer sae dear to me:
    O what blude's this upon your hand?
        O dear son, tell to me;
    It is the blude of my gay goss-hawk,
        He wadna flee for me.

15   O thy hawk's blude was neer sae red,
        Nor eer sae dear to me:
    O what blude's this upon your dirk?
        Dear Willie, tell to me;
    It is the blude of my ae brother,
        O dule and wae is me!

[1] The first eleven stanzas, which belong to the ballad of "The Twa Brothers," are not reprinted here.

16   O what will ye say to your father?
        Dear Willie, tell to me;
    I'll saddle my steed, and awa I'll ride,
        To dwell in some far countrie.

17   O when will ye come hame again?
        Dear Willie, tell to me;
    When sun and mune leap on yon hill,
        And that will never be.

18   She turnd hersel right round about,
        And her heart burst into three:
    My ae best son is deid and gane,
        And my tother ane I'll neer see.

GE F[1]

Child *English and Scottish Popular Ballads* I 442–43 No. 49F "The Twa Brothers" (the text is based on Buchan's and Motherwell's manuscripts).[2]

18   What blood is this upon you, William,
        And looks sae red on thee?
    It is the blood o my grey-hound,
        He wouldna run for me.

19   O that's nae like your grey-hound's blude,
        William, that I do see;
    I fear it is your own brother's blood
        That looks sae red on thee.

20   That is not my own brother's blude,
        Father, that ye do see;
    It is the blood o my good grey steed,
        He woudna carry me.

[1] Thanks are due Houghton Mifflin Co. for permission to reprint this text.

[2] The first seventeen stanzas, which belong to the ballad of "The Twa Brothers," are not reprinted here.

21   O that is nae your grey steed's blude,
      William, that I do see;
    It is the blood o your brother John,
      That looks sae red on thee.

22   It's nae the blood o my brother John,
      Father, that ye do see;
    It is the blude o my good grey hawk,
      Because he woudna flee.

23   O that is nae your grey hawk's blood,
      William, that I do see;
    Well, it's the blude o my brother,
      This country I maun flee.

24   O when will ye come back again,
      My dear son, tell to me?
    When sun and moon gae three times round,
      And this will never be.

25   Ohon, alas! now William, my son,
      This is bad news to me;
    Your brother's death I'll aye bewail,
      And the absence o thee.

GE G[1]

Child *English and Scottish Popular Ballads* I 443–44 No. 49G "The Twa Brothers" (from American oral tradition).[2]

6   What shall I tell your dear father,
      When I go home to-night?
    You'll tell him I'm dead and in my grave,
      For the truth must be told.

[1] Thanks are due Houghton Mifflin Co. for permission to reprint this text.

[2] The first five stanzas, which belong to the ballad of "The Twa Brothers," are not reprinted here.

7   What shall I tell your dear mother,
          When I go home to-night?
      You'll tell her I'm dead and in my grave,
          For the truth must be told.

8   How came this blood upon your knife?
          My son, come tell to me;
      It is the blood of a rabbit I have killed,
          O mother, pardon me.

9   The blood of a rabbit couldnt be so pure,
          My son, come tell to me;
      It is the blood of a squirrel I have killed,
          O mother, pardon me.

10   The blood of a squirrel couldnt be so pure,
          My son, come tell to me;
      It is the blood of a brother I have killed,
          O mother, pardon me.

GE H

Herd *Scottish Songs* I (1776) 91 (reprinted in Child *English and Scottish Popular Ballads* I 448 No. 51A).[1]

7   What ails thee, what ails thee, Geordy Wan,
        What ails thee sae fast to rin?
    For I see by thy ill colour
        Some fallow's deed thou hast done.

8   Some fallow's deed I have done, mother,
        And I pray you pardon me;
    For I've cutted aff my greyhound's head;
        He wadna rin for me.

[1] The first six stanzas, which belong to the ballad of "Lizie Wan," are not reprinted here.

9 Thy greyhound's bluid was never sae red,
    O my son Geordy Wan!
  For I see by thy ill colour
    Some fallow's deed thou hast done.

10 Some fallow's deed I hae done, mother,
    And I pray you pardon me;
  For I hae cutted aff Lizie Wan's head
    And her fair body in three.

11 O what wilt thou do when thy father comes hame,
    O my son Geordy Wan?
  I'll set my foot in a bottomless boat,
    And swim to the sea-ground.

12 And when will thou come hame again,
    O my son Geordy Wan?
  The sun and the moon shall dance on the green
    That night when I come hame.

GE I[1]

Child *English and Scottish Popular Ballads* I 448–49 No. 51B "Lizie Wan" (from Motherwell's manuscript).[2]

10 O what blude is that on the point o your knife,
    Dear son, come tell to me?
  It is my horse's, that I did kill,
    Dear mother and fair ladie.

11 The blude o your horse was neer sae red,
    Dear son, come tell to me;
  It is my grandfather's, that I hae killed,
    Dear mother and fair ladie.

[1] Thanks are due Houghton Mifflin Co. for permission to reprint this text.

[2] The first nine stanzas, which belong to the ballad of "Lizie Wan," are not reprinted here.

77

12 The blude of your grandfather was neer sae fresh,
  Dear son, come tell to me;
It is my sister's, that I did kill,
  Dear mother and fair ladie.

13 What will ye do when your father comes hame,
  Dear son, come tell to me?
I'll set my foot on yon shipboard,
  And I hope she'll sail wi me.

14 What will ye do wi your bonny bonny young wife,
  Dear son, come tell to me?
I'll set her foot on some other ship,
  And I hope she'll follow me.

15 And what will ye do wi your wee son,
  Dear son, come tell to me?
I'll leave him wi you, my dear mother,
  To keep in remembrance of me.

16 What will ye do wi your houses and lands,
  Dear son, come tell to me?
I'll leave them wi you, my dear mother,
  To keep my own babie.

17 And whan will you return again,
  Dear son, come tell to me?
When the sun and the mune meet on yon hill,
  And I hope that'll neer be.

GE J[1]

O. D. Campbell and C. J. Sharp *English Folksongs from the Southern Appalachians* (New York 1917) 26 No. 7A (with melody).

1   How come that blood on your shirt sleeve?
      Pray, son, now tell to me.
    It is the blood of the old greyhound
    That run young fox for me.

2   It is too pale for that old greyhound.
    It is the blood of the old grey mare
    That ploughed that corn for me.

3   It is too pale for that old grey mare.
    It is the blood of my youngest brother
    That hoed that corn for me.

4   What did you fall out about?
    Because he cut yon holly bush
    Which might have made a tree.

5   O what will you tell to your father dear
    When he comes home from town?
    I'll set my foot in yonder ship
    And sail the ocean round.

6   O what will you do with your sweet little wife?
    I'll set her foot in yonder ship
    To keep me company.

7   O what will you do with your three little babes?
    I'll leave them here in the care of you
    For to keep you company.

8   O what will you do with your house and land?
    I'll leave it here in care of you
    For to set my children free.

[1] Thanks are due G. P. Putnam's Sons for permission to reprint this text.

GE K[1]

O. D. Campbell and C. J. Sharp *English Folksongs from the Southern Appalachians* (New York 1917) 27 No. 7B (with melody).

1   O what will you say when your father comes back,
O what will you say to me?
I'll set my foot on yonder little boat,
I'll sail away over the sea,
I'll sail away over the sea.

GE L

As heard in Virginia by Mrs. T. P. Cross from her aunt, Mrs. B. D. Moncure. The ballad has been sung in the family for several generations.

1   What is that on your sword so red,
Dear son, pray tell unto me?
'Tis the blood of a gagillion,
Dear mother, pity me!
'Tis the blood of a gagillion,
Dear mother, pity me!

2   No gillion's blood was e'er so red,
Dear son, ...
'Tis the blood of my dear brother,
Dear mother, ...

3   What did you and your brother fall out about?
For cutting down a hazel-nut bush
That might have grown a tree.

4   What will you do when your father comes home?
I'll get aboard of yonder ship
And sail away to sea.

[1] Thanks are due G. P. Putnam's Sons for permission to reprint this text.

5   And when will you return, my son?
When the sun and the moon set on yonder hill,
And that will never be.

GE M[1]

C. J. Sharp *Folk-Songs of English Origin Collected in the Southern Appalachian Mountains* (a manuscript in the Harvard College Library) I 328; reprinted with minor variations, which are not accounted for in the Preface, in C. J. Sharp *American-English Folk-Songs* (1st ser. New York 1918) 2–7 No. 1.

1   What has came this blood on your shirt sleeve?
      O dear love, tell me.
This is the blood of the old grey horse
That plowed that field for me, me, me,
That plowed that field for me.

2   It does look too pale for the old grey horse
That plowed that field for you.

3   What has came this blood on your shirt sleeve?
This is the blood of the old grey hound
That traced that fox for me.

4   It does look too pale for the old grey hound
That traced that fox for you.

5   What has came this blood on your shirt sleeve?
This is the blood of my brother-in-law
That went away with me.

6   And it's what did you fall out about?
About a little bit of a bush
That soon would have made a tree.

[1] Thanks are due the Harvard College Library for permission to reprint this text.

7 An it's what will you do now, my love?
  I'll set my foot in yanders ship
  And I'll sail across the sea.

8 And it's when will you come back, my love?
  When the sun sets into yanders sycamore tree
  And it's that will never be.

GE N[1]

A. P. Hudson *Specimens of Mississippi Folklore* (Ann Arbor 1928)
6 No. 5 "The Cruel Brother."

1 What blood is that blood on your sleeve?
  My son, come tell it to me.[2]
  It is the blood of the old gray hound
  Who drove the fox for me.

2 The blood is too red for the blood of a hound.
  It is the blood of the old gray mare
  Who plowed the field for me.

3 The blood is too red for the blood of a mare.
  It is the blood of my little brother
  Who rode along with me.

4 What did you and your little brother fall out
   about?
  About a holly bush
   That might have been a tree.

5 What will you do when your good old father
   comes home?
  I'll go away from this country
  And sail across the sea.

---

[1] Thanks are due A. P. Hudson for permission to reprint this text.

[2] This refrain is omitted in the following stanzas.

6   What will you do with your pretty little house
          and lot?
       Give it to my good old father
          To bring up my children for me.

7   What will you do with your pretty little wife?
       I'll take her with me and sail away
          Across the deep blue sea.

GE O[1]

A. P. Hudson "Ballads and Songs from Mississippi" *Journal of American Folklore* XXXIX (1926) 93–94 No. 1 "Edward."

1   What made you kill your brother, my son,
       My son, pray tell it to me?[2]
       For cutting down that little bush
          Which might have made a tree.

2   What will you do when your father comes home?
       I'll put my foot on yonders boat
          And sail all over the sea.

3   What will you do with your children, my son?
       I'll leave them with you, dear mother,
          To keep you company.

4   What will you do with your house and land?
       I'll leave them here with you, dear mother,
          To set my children free.

5   What will you do with your wife, my son?
       I'll put her foot on yonders boat
          And let her sail with me.

[1] Thanks are due A. P. Hudson and the editor of the *Journal of American Folklore* for permission to reprint this text.

[2] This line is omitted in later stanzas.

6　　When are you coming home, my son?
　　　When the son goes down on yonders high hill,
　　　　Which you know that never shall be.

GE P[1]

A. K. Davis Jr. *Traditional Ballads of Virginia* (Cambridge 1929)
123 No. 7C "What is that on the end of your sword?"

1　　What is that on the end of your sword,
　　　　My dear son, tell to me?
　　　'Tis the blood of an English crow
　　　And I wish it had never been.

2　　Crow's blood was ne'er so red as that.
　　　'Tis the blood of my dear little brother,
　　　　And I wish it had never been.

3　　How did it happen?
　　　'Twas digging round the hollow tree,
　　　　And I wish it had never been.

4　　What will you do with your dear little son?
　　　I will leave him with his grandpapa
　　　　To make him think of me.

5　　What will you do with your dear little daughter?
　　　I will leave her with her grandmama
　　　　To make her think of me.

6　　What will you do with your dear little wife?
　　　She will put her foot on yonder boat
　　　　And sail away with me.

7　　When will you come back?
　　　When the sun and moon set on yonder hill
　　　　And that will never be.

[1] Thanks are due Arthur Kyle Davis, Jr., and the Harvard University Press for permission to reprint this text.

GE Q[1]

A. K. Davis Jr. *Traditional Ballads of Virginia* (Cambridge 1929) 121–23 No. 7B "What is that on the end of your sword?"

1   What is that on the end of your sword,
        My dear son, tell to me?
    What is that on the end of your sword,
    My dear son, tell to me?
    'Tis the very blood of an English crane
        My father sent to me.
    'Tis the very blood of an English crane
        My father sent to me.

2   Crane's blood is not so red.
    'Tis the very blood of my dear little brother,
        And I wish it had never been.

3   What will your father say to you?
    I will put my foot in the bottom of the boat
        And sail away to sea.

4   What will you do with your pretty little wife?
    She shall put her foot in the bottom of the boat
        And sail away with me.

5   What will you do with your dear little boy?
    I will leave him with his grandparents
        To make him think of me.

6   What will you do with your sweet little girl?
    I will leave her to her grandmother
        To make her think of me.

7   When do you expect to return again?
    When the sun and the moon set on yonder hill,
        And that will never be.

[1] Thanks are due Arthur Kyle Davis, Jr., and the Harvard University Press for permission to reprint this text.

GE R[1]

A. K. Davis Jr. *Traditional Ballads of Virginia* (Cambridge 1929) 121 (note to No. 7B). An unprinted text sung by Mrs. Susan Isham Blain. This text is the same as GE Q except for the conflation of stanzas 5 and 6 (the boy is left with his grandmother) and the reading "When the red sun sets on yonder hill" in the last stanza.

GE S[1]

A. K. Davis Jr. *Traditional Ballads of Virginia* (Cambridge 1929) 124 No. 7D.

1   What is that on your sword so red?
    Dear son, pray tell unto me.
 'Tis the blood of a gay gilleon.
    Dear mother, pity me.
 'Tis the blood of a gay gilleon.
    Dear mother, pity me.

2   No gilleon's blood was e'er so red.
 'Tis the blood of my dear brother.

3   What will you do when your father comes home?
 I'll get aboard of yonder ship
    And sail away to sea.

4   When will you return, my son?
 When the sun and the moon set on yonder hill,
    And that will never be.

[1] Thanks are due Arthur Kyle Davis, Jr., and the Harvard University Press for permission to reprint this text.

GE T[1]

A. K. Davis Jr. *Traditional Ballads of Virginia* (Cambridge 1929) 120–21 No. 7A "How come that red blood on your coat?"

1 How come that red blood on your coat?
   Pray, Son John, tell it to me.
   It is the blood of my fine horse
   That ran away with me.

2 How come that red blood on your coat?
   It is the blood of my fine gilligohound
   That trailed the track for me.

3 How come that red blood on your coat?
   It is the blood of my poor little brother
   That rode along with me.

4 What did you and your little brother fall out about?
   We fell out about a chestnut bush
   Which you might call a tree.

5 What will you do when your father comes home?
   I'll set my feet in yonders boat
   And sail cross the sea.

6 What will you do with your pretty little wife?
   I'll set her down by my side
   And sail across the sea.

7 What will you do with your sweet little baby?
   I'll set him down betwixt my knees
   And sail across the sea.

8 What will you do to get rid of the law?
   I'll set my feet in yonders boat
   And sail across the sea.

[1] Thanks are due Arthur Kyle Davis, Jr., and the Harvard University Press for permission to reprint this text.

9   When will you be back?
     When the sun and the moon set on yonders hill,
     And that will never be.

GE U[1]

A. K. Davis Jr. *Traditional Ballads of Virginia* (Cambridge 1929)
124 No. 7E.

1   Willie, my son, what have you done,
          With blood all over your clothes?
         He mumbled out with all his might,
          Been bleeding out of my nose.

GE V

Combs MS; see Kittredge *Journal of American Folklore* XXXIX
(1926) 93. I have not seen this text.

GE W

Perrow MS; see Kittredge *Journal of American Folklore* XXXIX
(1926) 93. I have not seen this text.

GE X

Shearin MS; see Shearin "British Ballads in the Cumberland Mountains" *Sewanee Review* XIX (1911) 316. I have not seen this text.

GE Y

Shearin and Combs MS; see H. G. Shearin and J. H. Combs *A
Syllabus of Kentucky Folksongs* ("Transylvania Studies in English")
[Lexington Ky., 1911] II 7. I have not seen this text.

GENERAL NOTE ON ENGLISH TEXTS.—It is perhaps worth saying that all
texts listed in the *Journal of American Folklore* XXVII (1914) 62; XXVIII
(1915) 200–202; and XXXIX (1926) 93 are accounted for in the preceding list.

[1] Thanks are due Arthur Kyle Davis, Jr., and the Harvard University Press
for permission to reprint this text.

GN

S. Grundtvig *Danmarks gamle Folkeviser* (Copenhagen 1895) VI 145
No. 340C. Taken down in Telemarken about the middle of the nine-
teenth century.

1   Hor hev du vori saa lengje?
             I Svenn i Rosensgaar!
          I enge hos drenge,
            kjær moder vaar;
          du venter mig sent eller aldrig!

2   Kvi er dit bryst saa blodigt?
          Folen meg trødde

3   Kvi er dit sverd saa blodigt?
          Jeg har dræbt min broder

4   Kvi rider du af veien?
          Jeg vil rømme af landet.

5   Naar kommer du tilbage?
          Naar stenene flyte

6   Naar flyter stenen?
          Naar fjærene søkke

7   Naar søkker fjæri?
          Naar ravnen den kvitnar

8   Naar kvitnar ravnen?
          Det sker dog aldrig.

GS A

Unfortunately this text, although of central importance, can no
longer be found; see references and incidental description of it in
Grundtvig *Danmarks gamle Folkeviser* VI (1895) 143–44.

GS B

E. G. Geijer and A. A. Afzelius *Svenska Folkvisor* (Stockholm 1880)
I 288 No. 54 I "Sven i Rosengård."

1 Hvar har du varit så länge,
  Du Sven i rosengård?
Jag har varit i stallet,
  Kära moder vår,
I vänten mig sent, men jag kommer aldrig!

2 Hvarför din kläder så blodig?
Hvita folan spjernte mig!

3 Hvarför är din skjorta så blodig?
Jag har mördat broder min.

4 Hvart skall du då ta' vägen?
Jag skall rymma af landet.

5 När kommer du tillbaka?
När korpen han hvitnar

6 Och när hvitnar korpen?
När gråsten han flyter.

GS C

E. G. Geijer and A. A. Afzelius *Svenska Folkvisor* (Stockholm 1880)
I 289–90 No. 54 2.

1 Hvar har du varit så länge,
  Sven i rosengård?
Jag har varit i stallet,
  Kära moder vår,
I vänten mig sent eller aldrig.

2 Hvad har du gjort i stallet?
Jag har vattnat fålarna.

3   Hvi är din fot så blodig?
         Svarta fålan trampa' mig.

4   Hvi är ditt svärd så blodigt?
         Jag har slagit min broder.

5   Hvart skall du då ta' vägen?
         Jag skall rymma af landet.

6   Hvad gör du då af din hustru?
         Hon får spinna för födan.

7   Hvar gör du då af barnen små?
         De få gå för hvars mans dörr.

8   När kommer du tillbaka?
         När svanen han svartnar.

9   Och när svartnar svanen?
         När korpen han hvitnar.

10   Och när hvitnar korpen?
         När gråstenen flyter.

11   Och när flyter gråsten?
         Stenen flyter aldrig.

GS D

A. I. Arwidsson *Svenska Fornsånger* II (1837) 83–85 No. 87A "Sven i Rosengård." From Småland. A. I. Ståhl (*Äldre och nyare svenska folkvisor* [Stockholm 1855] I 11 No. 12) prints this text without acknowledgment and assigns it to Finland.

1   Hvar har du va't så länge?
       Sven i Rosengård!
    Jo, jag har va't i stallet.
      Kära moder vår;
    J vänta mig sent eller aldrig!

2   Hvad har du gjort i stallet?
     Jo, jag har skådat blacken.

3   Hur är din fot så blodig?
     Jo, blacken har mig tradat.

4   Hur är ditt svärd så blodigt?
     Jag har stuckit ihjäl min broder!

5   Hvar har du gjort af brodren din?
     Han ligger utom stallsvägg!

6   Hvad skall du nu ha för det?
     Jo, jag skall rymma af landet.

7   Hvad skall du göra af hustrun din?
     Den sätter jag pa sörje-skrin.

8   Hvad skall du göra af barnen din?
     De få lita vänner och fränder till.

9   Hvad skall du göra af kreaturen?
     Dem släpper jag på sjelfföda.

10   Hvad skall du göra af åker och äng?
     Dem lägger för fäfot.

11   När skall jag vänta dig igen?
     När korpen han hvitnar.

12   När hvitnar korpen?
     När svanen han svartnar.

13   När svartnar svanen?
     När stenen han flyter.

14   När flyter stenen?
     När fjädern han sjunker.

15   När sjunker fjädern?
      När alla enbär mogna.

16   När mogna alla enebär?
      När alla pigor bli gifta.

17   När bli alla pigor gifta?
      När kyrkan blifver enka.

18   När blir kyrkan enka?
      Jo, innan verldens ända.

GS E

A. I. Arwidsson *Svenska Fornsånger* (Stockholm 1837) II 86–87 No.
87B "Sven i Rosengård." From Östergötland.

1   Hvar har du va't så länge?
        Sven i Rosengard!
     Jag har va't i stallet.
        Kära moder vår;
        J vänten mig sent eller aldrig!

2   Hvad har du gjort i stallet?
     Jag har vatnat fålar alla.

3   Hvi är ditt svärd så blodigt?
     Jag slog ihjäl min broder.

4   Hvad vill du nu då göra?
     Jag rymmer utaf landet.

5   Hvar vill du göra af hustru och barn?
     De få gå verlden af och an.

6   När får jag dig hemvänta?
     När kyrkan blir enka.

7   När blir kyrkan enka?
     När der är inga bänkar.

8   När får jag dig hemvänta?
       När alla fjädrar sjunka.

9   Och när sjunker fjädern?
       När jernet det flyter.

10   När får jag dig hemvänta?
       När korpen blir hviter.

11   När blir korpen hviter?
       När svanen blir svarter.

12   När får jag dig hemvänta?
       När alla enbär mogna.

13   När mogna alla enebär?
       När alla flickor bli gifta.

14   När får jag dig hemvänta?
       När tallen han löfgas.

15   När löfgas tallen?
       När björken has barras.

16   Hvar vill du göra af åker och äng?
       Den får bli utan hägn och stägn.

GS F

Thomasson "Visor upptecknade i Kyrkhults socken i Bleking"
Nyare bidrag till kännedom om de svenska landsmålen VII Part VI (1890)
16–17 No. 9 "Sven i Rosengård."

1   Hvar har du vatt så länge,
          Sven i Rosengård?
       Jag har vatt i stallet,
          Kära moder vår,
          I vänten mig sent eller aldrig.

2   Hvad har du gjort i stallet?
       Jag har ryktat hästen.

3   Hur är din sko så blodig?
        Jo hästen har mig trampat.

4   Hur är ditt svärd så blodigt?
        Jag har stuckit ihjäl min broder.

5   Hvar har du gjort af din broder?
        Han ligger bakom stallen.

6   Hvad skall du nu ha för det?
        Jo jag skall rymma af landet.

7   Hvad skall du göra af hustru din?
        Den sätter jag på sörjeskrin.

8   Hvad skall du göra af barnen din?
        De få lita fränder ock vänner till.

9   Hvad skall det bli af kreaturen din?
        Dem släpper jag pa ängen grön.

10   Hvad skall det bli af åkren din?
        Den läger jag för fäfot.

11   När skall jag vänta dig hem?
        När som korpen han hvitnar.

12   När hvitnar korpen?
        När som svanen svartnar.

13   När svartnar svanen?
        När stenen han flyter.

14   När flyter stenen?
        När fjädern hon sjunker.

15   När sjunker fjädern?
        När alla enbär mogna.

16   När mogna alla enbär?
         Da alla flickor bli gifta.

17   När bli alla flickor gifta?
         Da kyrkan blifver änka.

18   När blir kyrkan änka?
         Jo vid värdens ända.

GS G

Bidrag till Södermanlands äldre kulturhistoria I Part I (1884) 32 No. 8 "Sven i Rosengård."

Hvar har du va't så länge,
Sven i rosengård?
Jo jag har va't i stallet,
Kära moder vår;
I vänten mig sent eller aldrig.

GS H

Bidrag till Södermanlands äldre kulturhistoria I Part III (1882) 37–38 "Sven i Rosengård."

1   Hvar har du varit så länge,
         Sven i Rosengård?
         Jag har varit i stallet,
         Kära moder vår!
         I vänten mig sent eller aldrig!

2   Hur har du blifvit så blodig,
         Blacka hästen trampade mig.

3   Hvart skall du då ta vägen?
         Jag skall rymma af landet.

4   När kommer du tillbaka?
         När som svanen svartnar.

5   När svartnar svanen?
               När som korpen hvitnar.

6   När hvitnar korpen?
               När som fjädern sjunker.

7   När sjunker fjädern?
               När som stenen flyter.

8   När flyter stenen?
               När som domen kommer.

GS J

Bidrag till Södermanlands äldre kulturhistoria II Part V (1884) 12–14
"Sven i Rosengård."

1   Hvar har du varit så länge,
               Du Sven i Rosengård?
           Jag har varit åt stallet,
               Kära moder vår!
           I vänten mig sent eller aldrig!

2   Hvad har du gjort åt stallet?
           Jag har vattnat hästarna.

3   Hvad har du fått på rocken?
           Hästen min har trampat mig.

4   Hvad har du fått pa skjortan?
           Jag har slagtat min syster.

5   Hvad skall du ha för detta?
           Jag skall rymma ur riket.

6   När kommer du tillbaka?
           När som tallcn bar löfven.

7   När bär då tallen löfven?
           Jo, när som alen barrar.

8   Och när då barrar alen?
    Jo, när som gråsten flyter.

9   Och när då flyter gråsten?
    Jo, när som fjädern sjunker.

10   Och när då sjunker fjädern?
    Jo, när som svanen svartnar.

11   Och när då svartnar svanen?
    Jo, när som korpen hvitnar.

GS K

"Svend i Rosengaard." MS J. P. Johannson, copy in S. Grundtvig's MSS, No. 64 in Dansk Folkemindesamling in the Royal Library, Copenhagen. From Østergøtland.

1   Hvor har du va'tt så länge?
    Du Sven i Rosengard!
   Jag har vatt ut stallet,
    kär moder var!
   Ni vänten mig sent heller aldrig!

2   Hvad har du gjort ut stallet?
    Jag har vattnat hästa.

3   Hvad har fått på byxera?
    Hästen ha tramp ma.

4   Hvad har du fått på skjurta?
    Ja ha slakte syster!

5   Hvad skall du ha för [det]?
    Jag skall rymma ur riket.

6   När kommer du igen?
    När allän barrar!

7   När barrs allän?
    När gråsten flyter.

8   När flyter gråsten?
            När fjädren sjunker.

9   När sjunker fjädren?
            När svanen svartnar.

10   När svartnar svanen?
            När korpen hvitnar.

GS L

"Sven i Rosengård." From Småland. MS Vs. 3:3 (II 2.B.6) of the Royal Library in Stockholm.

1   Hvad har du fått för blod på foten,
            Sven i Rosengård?
            Jo fålarne ha trampat mig,
            Kära moder var.
            I vänten mig sent eller aldrig.

2   Hvad har du fått för blod på handen?
            Jag har stungit ihel min yngsta Broder.

3   Hvart vill du fly och vandra?
            Den ingen mig kan klandra.

4   När kommer du igen då?
            När dagarne få ända.

5   När få dagarne ända?
            När verlden blir till intet.

6   När blir verlden till intet?
            När vi skall fram för domen.

7   Hvad får du i domen?
            Förbannelse och mörker.

8   Da sörjer jag till döda.
            En annan skall ni föda.

GS M

From Småland. The following variants are written in the text of
GS L. I follow the stanza numbering in the copy made for me.

4 Hvi är ditt svärd så rostigt?
   Jag har förrådt min syster.

6 Hvad vill du göra af hustrun din?
   Jo, jag vill ta 'na med mig.

8 Hvad vill du göra af mor din?
   Jo, hon får sitta i vrå och fälla tår.

9 När skall vi dig då vänta?
   När alla klockor klämta.

12 När flyter grå-stenen?
    När solen går upp vestan.

13 När går sol upp vestan?
    När hon går ned östan.

14 När går sol ned östan,
        Du Sven i Rosengård?
    Aldrig före Dome-dagen,
        Kära moder min.
    Ni vänten mig sent, men jag kommer aldrig.

GS N

"Sven i Rosengård." From Bohuslän. Västsvenska Folkminnes-
föreningen Acc. No. 205 7–8. Sung by Tilda Johansson, Finsbo, in
1921. I have regulated stops.

1 Å var har du nu varit, ja Sven i Rosengård?
   Jo jag har vattnat fålarna, ja kära moder vår.

2 Varför är ditt svärd så blodigt?
   Jo jag har slagit min broder.

3 Var skall du taga vägen?
  Jo jag skall rymma ur landet.

4 Å var ska bli av din hustru?
  ja hon far spinna för födan sin.

5 Var ska bli av dina barn de små?
  Ja de får gå för var mans dörr.

6 När kommer du tillbaka?
  När korpen den vitnar.

7 När vitnar korpen?
  När svanen den svartnar.

8 När svartnar svanen?
  När gråstenen flyter.

9 När flyter gråstenen?
  Gråstenen flyter aldrig.

GSF A

Svenska literatursällskapet i Finland (Helsingfors) MS 1 125 "Sven i Rosengård."

1 Var haver du varit så länge, du Sven i rosengård?
  Jag haver varit i stallet, kära moder vår.
  —I vänten mig sent eller aldrig.—

2 Vad haver du gjort i stallet så länge?
  Jag haver skrapat blacken.

3 Du är så blodiger på din hand?
  Ja, fålan haver bitit mig.

4 Du är så blodiger på din arm?
  Ja, fålan haver slagit mig.

5 Du är så blodiger på ditt svärd?
  Ja, jag haver slagit hjäl min bror.

6   Vart skall du taga vägen?
     Jag måste rymma landet.

7   Vad skall du göra av åker och äng?
     De måste ju ligga för var mans fe.

8   Vad skall du göra av kreaturen din?
     De måste ju också stickas ihjäl.

9   Vad skall du göra av din hus och knut?
     Di får ju väl ruttna knut från knut.

10 Vad skall du göra av barnen din?
     De få väl stå vid andras dörr.

11 Vad skall du göra utav hustrun (din)?
     Hon får väl spinna för födan sin.

12 När skall du komma tillbaka igen?
     När korpen börjar att vitna.

13 När börjar korpen att vitna?
     När som svanen svartnar.

14 När börjar svanan att svartna?
     När stenarna börja att flyta.

15 När skall stenen flyta?
     När fjäddran börjar att sjunka.

16 När börjar fjäddran att sjunka, du Sven i rosengård?
     När som domen kommer, kära moder vår.
     —I vänten mig sent eller aldrig.—

GSF B

Svenska literatursällskapet i Finland (Helsingfors) MS Joukahainen
IX 263 "Sven i Rosengård."

1   Var haver du varit så länge, Sven i rosengård?
     I stallet har jag varit, kära moder vår.

2   Vad haver du gjort i stallet?
Jag har ryktat brunan.

3   Var har du blodat rocken din?
Brunan har sparkat mig på magen.

4   Var har du blodat skjortan din?
Jag har stuckit min broder.

5   Vart skall du taga vägen?
Jag måste rymma ur landet.

6   Vad skall du göra utav din gamla fader?
Han måste föda sig med yxen.

7   Vad skall du göra utav din moder?
Hon måste föda sig med tenen.

8   Vad skall du göra utav din hustru?
Hon måste taga sig en annan.

9   Vad skall du göra av din' små barn?
De måste stå och fälla tår på tår.

10   Vad skall du göra av din åker och äng?
De måste falla under fäfot.

11   Vad skall du göra utav din' hus?
De måste rottna knut för knut.

12   Vad skall du göra av din' penningar?
Dem giver jag åt vänner och grannar.

13   När kommer du åter igen, Sven i rosengård?
När björken baras, kära moder vår.
—I vänten mig sent eller aldrig.—

14   När baras då björken?
När granen lövas.

15 När lövas då granen?
 När korpen vitnar.

16 När vitnar då korpen?
 När svanen svartnar.

17 När svartnar då svanen?
 När fjädren sjunker.

18 När sjunker då fjädren?
 När stenen flyter.

19 När flyter då stenen, Sven i rosengård?
 På den yttersta dagen, kära moder vår.

GSF C

Svenska literatursällskapet i Finland (Helsingfors) MS Svensson 6
29 "Sven i Rosengård."

1 Vart haver du varit så länge, du sven i rosendegård?
 Jag har varit vid sjöastrand, allra kär moderen vår.
 —I vänten mig sent eller aldrig.—

2 Hur är du så blodiger om din hand?
 Hästen haver ju sparkat mig.

3 Hur är du så blodiger om ditt svärd?
 Jag haver ju slagit min broder ihjäl.

4 Vart tänker du taga vägen då?
 Jag haver ju tänkt att rymma bort.

5 Vad skall du göra av de barnen små?
 De få gå för andras dör att söka där sitt bröd.

6 Vad skall du göra av din hustru då?
 Hon får ju arbeta för födan sin.

7 Vad skall du göra med din trogna hund?
   Honom jag tager med på vandringen min.

8 När tänker du komma tillbaka då?
   När stjärnorna dansa på himlen blå.

9 När börja stjärnorna dansa på himlen blå?
   När gråstenen flyter på vattnen.

10 När flyter gråstenen på vattnen?
   När korpen han vitnar och svanen blir blå.

11 När vitnar korpen och när blånar svanen?
   När solen den svartnar.

12 Och när svartnar solen?
   När himlens klockor klämta.

13 När klämta himlens klockor, du sven i rosendegård?
   När domsbasunen klingar, allra kär moderen vår.
   —I vänten mig sent eller aldrig.—

GSF D
Bygdeminnen II iv "Sven i Rosengård."

1 Var haver du varit så länge, Sven i rosengård?
   Jag haver ju varit i stallet, kära moder vår.

2 Vad haver du gjort i stallet?
   Jag haver ju skrapat Blacken.

3 Var haver du blodat ner skjortan din?
   Jo, Blacken slog mig på magen.

4 Var har du gjort av din broder?
   Jag haver ju stuckit ihjäl en.

5 Vad skall du med de små barnen?
   De måste väl komma i annan mans vård.

6   Vad skall du med dina vackra hus?
De måste väl falla knut från knut.

7   När kommer du sen tillbaka?
När svarta korpen han ljusnar.

8   När ljusnar svarta korpen?
När stjärnan faller till jorden.

9   När faller stjärnan till jorden?
När domens dagar stunda.

GSF E

Svenska literatursällskapet i Finland (Helsingfors) MS 10 451 "Sven i Rosengård."

1   Vart haver du varit så länge?
—du Sven i roser vår.—
Jag har varit i stallet, klappat blacken.
—I ömma moder vår.—

2   Var haver du blodat din skjorta?
Blacken haver sparkat mig på magen.

3   Var haver du blodat din värja?
Jag har stuckit ihjäl min broder.

4   Vart skall du nu taga vägen?
Jag tänker att upp åt landet.

5   När kommer du hem tillbaka?
När som gråstenen flyter på vattnet.

6   När flyter då gråsten på vattnet?
När som granarna bliva med löven.

7   När bliver då granar med löven?
När som björkarna bliva med barren.

8   När bliver då björkar med barren?
När som alla flickor bliver gifta.

9   När bliver då alla flickor gifta?
Uppå den stora domedagen.

10   När kommer den stora domedagen?
—du Sven i roser vår.—
Uppå den yttersta dagen.
—I ömma moder vår.—

GSF F

Svenska literatursällskapet i Finland (Helsingfors) MS 47 52. No title.

1   Var har du blodat din skjorta,
du tvenne rosen god?
Bru haver mig sparkat,
du kära moder vår.

2   Var har du blodat ditt svärd?
Jag har stuckit min broder.

3   Vart skall du taga vägen?
Jag måste rymma landet.

4   När skall du komma hem?
När svanen hon svartnar.

5   När svartnar då svanen?
När korpen han vitnar.

6   När vitnar korpen då?
När stenen han flyter.

GSF G

Svenska literatursällskapet i Finland (Helsingfors) MS Svensson
6 29 "Sven i Rosengård."

1   Vart haver du varit så länge
   du sven i rosendegård?
   Jag har varit vid sjöastrand,
   vid sjöstrand, kär moderen min.
   —I vänten mig sent eller aldrig.—

2   Vad gjorde du vid sjöastrand?
   Jag har vattnat fålan min.

3   Vi är din hand så blodig?
   Grå hästen han har sparkat mig.

4   Vi är ditt svärd så blodigt?
   Jag har slagit min broder ihjäl.

5   Vad skall du göra här?
   Jag skall nu i landsflykt gånga.

GSF H

Svenska literatursällskapet i Finland (Helsingfors) MS Rancken 274.
No title.

1 Var haver du varit så länge
  —du sven i rosenvård?
  Jag har varit i stallet och skrapa Blacken,
  —I ömma moders vård.

2 Var haver du blodat din skjorta?
  Blacken har sparkat mig i magen.

3 Var haver du blodat din värja?
  Jag har ihjälstuckit min broder.

4   Vart skall du taga vägen?
     Jag har tänkt att ge mig på landet.

5   När kommer du hem tillbaka?
     När som granarna bliva med löve.

6   När kommer du hem tillbaka?
     När som björkarna bliva med bare.

7   När kommer du hem tillbaka?
     När som korparna bliva vita.

8   När kommer du hem tillbaka?
     När som svanorna bliva svarta.

9   När kommer du hem tillbaka?
     När som alla flickor bliva gifta.

10   När bliva då alla flickor gifta?
     Uppå den stora dagen.

11   När är den stora dagen,
     —du sven i rosenvård.—
     Uppå den stora domedagen
     —I ömma moders vård.—

GSF J

Svenska literatursällskapet i Finland (Helsingfors) MS R 3 B VIII
155 "Sven i Rosengård."

1   Var har du varit så länge—du sven i rosengård—
     Jag har varit i stallet—kära moder vår—
     —I vänten mig sent eller aldrig.

2   Vad haver du gjort i stallet?
     Jag haver stuckit min broder ihäl (ihjäl).

3   Vart skall du taga vägen?
     Jag måste väl rymma landet.

4   Vart skall du göra av hustrun din?
     Hon får väl spinna för födan sin.

5   Vart skall du göra av barnen?
     De måste väl gå för andra mans dörr.
     (De måste väl tigga födan sin.)

6   Vart skall du av åkren din?
     Han får väl falla lind på lind.

7   När skall du komma tillbaka?
     När svanen börjar svartna.

8   När börjar svanen svartna?
     När korpen börjar vitna.

9   När börjar korpen vitna?
     När stenen börjar flyta.

10   När börjar stenen flyta?
     —du sven i rosengård.—
     När solen går upp i väster
     —kära moder vår.—
     —I vänten mig sent eller aldrig.—

A SWEDISH BROADSIDE BASED UPON "SVEN I ROSENGÅRD"

This text is printed from *Fyra Stycken Nya Och Lustiga Wisor* (Götheborg: tryckt hos Samuel Norberg 1794).

1   Huru är du blefwen gifter, du Daniel ungerswän?
     Det war som det kunde å ja jamen,
     Det war som det kunde å ja jamen.

2   Hwar ligger då din unga Brud?
     I höga loft på bolstrar blå.

3 Hwar ligger du då sjelfwer?
  I laden uppå hö och strå.

4 Hwad äter då din unga Brud?
  Äggemat på silfwerfat.

5 Hwad äter du då sjelfwer?
  Sille-rump och hafrestump.

6 Hwad dricker då din unga Brud?
  Öhl och mjöd och bästa win.

7 Hwad dricker då du sjelfwer?
  Drickat är surt och wärre ä lut.

8 Hwem dantsar med din unga Brud?
  Alla wåra Prästasöner.

9 Med hwem dantsar du då sjelfwer?
  Med Kärringer och häxor.

www.ingramcontent.com/pod-product-compliance
Lightning Source LLC
Chambersburg PA
CBHW071131250626
47159CB00006B/2202